Understanding and Negotiating 360° (Ancillary Rights) Deals

Understanding and Negotiating 360° (Ancillary Rights) Deals

Kendall A. Minter, Esq.

Nam Chi, L.L.C.
Stone Mountain, Georgia

UNDERSTANDING AND NEGOTIATING
360° (Ancillary Rights) DEALS
By Kendall A. Minter, Esq.

Exclusive Publisher: Nam Chi, L.L.C.
5398 East Mountain Street
Stone Mountain, Georgia   30083
Phone: 1.770.879-7400
Fax: 1.770.879-5695
Email: kamlaw@aol.com
Website: www.askmusiclawyer.com

Kendall A. Minter, Publisher / Editorial Director
Yvonne Rose/Quality Press, Production Coordinator
Printed Page, Interior Designer
Namik Minter Hawkins, Cover Designer
Author Photos, Sandra Lewis Glass

The publication is designed to provide accurate and authoritative information in regard to the subject matter covered. It is sold with the understanding that the publisher is not engaged in rendering legal, accounting or other professional services through this book. If legal advice or other expert assistance is required, the services of a competent professional should be sought.

Paperback ISBN #: 978-0-9961790-0-3
Library of Congress Control #: 2015935755.

Printed in the United States of America

Table of Contents

Acknowledgements

This, my first book, has been ten years in the making and began with an intended focus on music industry deals, structure, competition and content. Outlines were written, scrapped and reborn. Research was started, stopped and then updated. Then, the business structure of the music industry went through a cataclysmic shift and most of the old business and deal paradigms went out the window, along with CD sales.

With the steady decline in traditional music sales, the merger and acquisition frenzy of the major labels and music publishers and the reemergence of the independent artist and label sector, it was clear that there was an increasing need to demystify and understand the new evolving music business models.

Thus, between continuous client demands, extensive time commitments to several non-profit music industry Boards of Directors, family time and life, I decided it was time to put to print my observations, experience and recommendations concerning the new music business deal models.

In navigating this literary journey, my path was propelled by my wife, Pamela's, frequent query "what have you done on your book today?"; my daughters', Kamali, Namik and Amani, regular encouragement to "get it done"; clients who confirmed the need for an industry primer; and the energy, focus and direction provided by the universal spirit to set goals and work my plan.

I want to also acknowledge my office right hand of over 25 years, my office manager, Louise Ferguson, who helps to keep it all together as well as my interns Lauren Frazier and Ronel Salter for their research assistance. To Garnett "Nas" Smith and Chuck Williams for their investments to help facilitate this project. To my longtime friend, Tony Rose, for paving the way to the world of quality self-publication.

We are all connected by differing strands of DNA, genealogy and energy and it is my hope that the information shared in the pages that follow connect with your pursuit of knowledge and information to better yourself and those in your personal and business spaces.

Preface

I've spent over thirty-five years as an entertainment lawyer, business advisor, peacemaker, deal negotiator and institution builder. During that time, I've been blessed to have the opportunity to represent, work with and spend time with international entertainment icons such as:

- Lena Horne
- Stevie Wonder
- Kirk Franklin
- Third World
- Ashanti
- Bonnie Raitt
- Ray Charles
- Roy Ayers
- Peter Tosh
- Bunny Wailer
- Jermaine Dupri
- MC Lyte
- Cassandra Wilson
- Dionne Warwick
- Musiq Soulchild
- Teddy Riley & Guy
- Eddie Levert
- Hugh Masekela

and scores of other celebrities, power broker industry executives such as:

- L. A. Reid
- Sylvia Rhone
- LeBaron Taylor
- Jim Fifield
- Ahmet Ertegun
- Bruce Lundvall
- Big Jon Platt
- Dr. George Butler
- Clarence Avant
- Steve Ross

- Russell Simmons
- Chris Blackwell
- Neil Portnow
- Frances Preston
- Tom Silverman

Hard-hitting athletes such as:
Evander Holyfield   WBO Heavyweight Champ Ray Mercer
International dignitaries, politicians and humanitarians such as:

- Archbishop Desmond Tutu
- Prime Minister Edward Seaga
- Dick Gregory
- Jamaican Senator and Former Minister of Sports Youth & Culture – Babsy Grange
- Mayor David Dinkins
- Mayor Maynard Jackson
- Mayor Kasim Reed
- Congressman Hank Johnson
- Congressman John Conyers
- Congresswoman Sheila Jackson Lee
- Georgia Attorney General Thurbert Baker
- Jesse Jackson

and a diverse array of songwriters, producers, filmmakers, actors, models, entrepreneurs, artist managers, radio announcers, musicians, singers and just plain folk with a dream and the spirit to work towards that dream's realization.

I've had numerous opportunities to help lay the groundwork for non-profit organizations whose primary missions are to provide assistance (financial and otherwise), professional networking, career education, and sustainable institutions helping others. My non-profit board work has included:

- The Black Entertainment & Sports Lawyers Association (Co-Founder and Director)
  www.besla.org

- The Rhythm & Blues Foundation
  (Founding Director Chairman and General Chairman Emeritus)
  www.rhythmblues.org

- The Living Legends Foundation
  (Director and General Counsel)
  www.livinglegendsfoundation.com

- SoundExchange
  (Director)
  www.soundexchange.com

My desire to educate and share information with others from our "next generation" has led me to teaching positions at:
- Benjamin Cardoza School of Law (Adjunct Professor)
- Georgia State University (Instructor)

This book is intended to share knowledge and information with anyone in the music industry who is seeking to empower themselves, be aware of current negotiating points and issues in the new business model recording deals and enhance their career.

My video on YouTube is the #1 most viewed video online worldwide that speaks specifically to understanding and negotiating 360° or ancillary rights deals; and it's due to that viewership that I decided to write this book. It picks up where the introductory video leaves off and provides valuable insight into specific negotiating points and strategies.

Now it's your turn to share the knowledge, pass it on and pay it forward.

Introduction

Since the turn of the new millennium clock in 2000, sales of CDs and other physical configurations of recorded music have declined steadily and annually by 5% - 11% in volume worldwide; due primarily to the dramatic increase in free online file sharing of music, illegal downloads and competing entertainment products, i.e.: video games, movies, concerts, DVDs, etc. This gradual but consistent slide downward has continued and beginning in 2011, sales of digital music began to outpace sales of CDs. Additionally, millions of illegal downloads significantly eroded legal sales and while legal digital downloads, purchased through i-tunes, Amazon.com and other online retailers have continued to increase annually, they have not yet equaled or replaced the loss in dollar value of physical sales.

As a result of the erosion of traditional music sales and corresponding revenue, record companies have begun to look for new business in models which would provide them with additional and non-traditional streams of income.

The 360° deal, also known as an ancillary rights or multiple rights or passive income participation deal is the new and now standard business model between the artist and music company, which grants the company an economic interest and sometimes controlling rights to the artist's non-record activities in the entertainment industry, including touring, merchandising, film, television, book publishing deals, product endorsements, licensing, online fan clubs and website ads, live theater and publishing.

All major and most independent record companies are now including 360° provisions in their new and mid-level artist deals. Understanding the intricacies of these provisions and how to negotiate and navigate them is essential for any artist seeking to enter into a recording contract.

The economics underlying ancillary rights deals will definitely impact an artist's financial bottom line and can make the difference between maintaining a profitable career or barely breaking even. Additionally, given the fact that the typical exclusive recording agreement provides for up to five or six albums to be delivered to the label, a contract which runs its full term could easily last for between 6-8 years. Many new artists today, if they are fortunate and in the top 5% in sales, may have a good 5-10 year career run. Therefore, it's critical to make sure that your royalty and music related earnings are maximized.

This book will examine the evolution of the 360° deal, the scope of rights covered and key points to negotiate in order to minimize or reduce the flow of profits out of an artist's pocket.

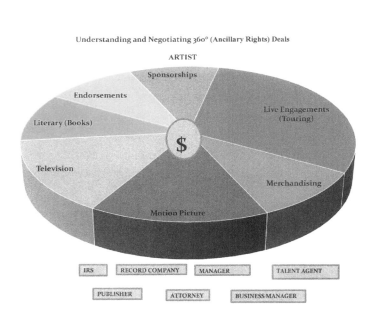

Chapter 1

Evolution of the 360° or Ancillary Rights Deal

The first generally reported 360° deal of significance was the deal with Robbi Williams set the template for future multiple rights deals. EMI followed the Robbi Williams deal with a similar deal for a term of five years with the group "Korn" a few months later. At a price tag estimated at $15 million, EMI acquired rights to a 30% share in the revenue streams earned by Korn in touring, merchandising, licensing and music publishing, as reported by Billboard magazine.

In 2005, Atlantic Records entered the multiple rights game with its signing of a 360 deal with the group "Paramore" for an estimated $200,000. Under this deal, Atlantic acquired a 30% stake in the group's net income from its activities in the areas of touring, merchandising, fan clubs and endorsements.

Also in 2005 Disney began to expand its deals with its actors/artists by securing multiple rights. This formula made perfect business sense for a company like Disney which has multiple overlapping divisions including film, TV, music, merchandising, live engagements and music publishing. Actually, a company like Disney which is fully vertically integrated is in a better position than a traditional record company to offer its artists value and opportunity in all of the key areas covered by multiple rights deals. For example, Disney owns ABC TV, the Disney Channel (on cable and satellite), Disney Radio, Disney Consumer Products (a merchandising company), Buena Vista Concerts (a live touring company), Hollywood

Records and Walt Disney Records, several music publishing companies and theme parks worldwide. Disney's signings included Jesse McCartney, Selena Gomez, and Demi Lovato. Occasionally, prior to signing an artist to a multiple rights deal, Disney has worked with several of its artists in one or more areas first before expanding their relationship. Miley Cyrus was initially introduced to the public through the popular show "Hannah Montana". The TV show debuted in March 2006 and later that Fall, a soundtrack album was released to critical acclaim which catapulted Miley to fast track stardom. Miley released her first solo album on Hollywood Records in June 2007. Since that time, she's gone on to sell millions of albums and has consistently hit the top of the Billboard album charts.

The Miley model was somewhat duplicated with Disney's development of acting/singing phenom Zendaya Coleman. Zendaya was initially signed as an actor, similar to Miley, and co-stars in Disney's hit TV show "Shake It Up". In 2012, Disney expanded its relationship with Zendaya by signing her to a multiple album recording and co-publishing deal (negotiated by yours truly). Zendaya expanded her brand and audience by capturing a coveted spot in the season 16 of ABC's hot show Dancing With the Stars, where she was the youngest contestant ever to appear on the show.

Soon after EMI implemented its joint venture deal structure, the other major labels began to experiment with their own incarnations of multiple rights deals. Additionally, powerhouse live concert promoter and venue owner Live Nation saw an opportunity to partner with some of the world's leading artists with whom it had existing touring relationships.

In October, 2007, Live Nation entered the 360 joint venture arena with its signing of a 10 year multiple rights deal with Madonna, valued at between $120-$150 million. The agreement with Madonna captured a broad swath of rights including recording (3 albums), touring, merchandising, fan clubs, music related TV projects and sponsorships. It has been reported that the deal with Madonna gives Live Nation a 10% stake in her touring revenue, 30% of her merchandising revenue and 50% of her licensing revenue.

Several other high value marquis signings followed in 2008 with U2 signing for $120 million in March 2008, Jay Z in April 2008 in a 10 year deal valued at $150 million, Shakira in July 2008 for a 10 year deal valued at between $70-$100 million and Nickelback in July 2008 in a deal valued at between $50-$70 million.

The deal with U2 included rights to touring, merchandising and the U2.com website. Jay-Z's deal encompasses the joint venture funding of start-up entertainment company, Roc Nation, recording, music publishing, merchandise and an artist/talent consulting and management division. Jay-Z's deal provides the artist/entrepreneur with financing and infrastructure necessary to significantly expand his brand across multiple entertainment industry platforms. It's reported that Jay's deal includes $5 million per year for his overhead for a 5 year period, a $25 million signing advance, $25 million in financing for acquisitions and investments, $10 million per album for three albums and another $45 million in general advances for touring, publishing, licensing and other rights.

The Nickelback deal with Live Nation varied the fixed time formula by defining the term as three album and touring cycles with an option for a fourth. A typical album cycle can run anywhere from 12 months to several years depending on how frequently an artist delivers and releases an album. A successful album can see an artist touring in support of that album for easily 1-2 years after its release. Recording schedules can stretch well beyond a year for some artists and can be as short as 4-6 months for others. Thus, an "album and touring cycle" can vary widely from artist to artist. The scope of rights acquired under the Nickelback deal is very broad and includes recordings, touring, sponsorships, merchandising, endorsements, DVDs, fan clubs, literary rights, website rights, broadcast rights and apparel.

By 2007, all of the (then 4 major labels—Sony Music Entertainment, Warner Music Group, EMI and Universal Music Group) and many of the well-established independent labels were requiring all new artists to grant them multiple rights without any additional advances as a standard provision in their exclusive recording agreements. One major label—Atlantic Records—developed extensive stand-alone contracts which covered fan clubs, touring and merchandising rights. The customary rights and ancillary income streams covered are:

- touring
- merchandising
- endorsements and sponsorships
- television
- motion picture

- literary (book publishing)
- publishing (in some cases)

The range of revenue acquired by the record labels varies widely and can be as little as 5% to as much as 30%. However, the typical range for the label's revenue share is 15% - 20%. How this share is calculated also varies from label to label and quite often from contract to contract. Certain revenue streams are calculated on the gross income payable to the artist without any deductions, such as endorsements, sponsorships, merchandising, television, literary and motion picture. The calculations for touring and live engagements are frequently more involved as deductions for certain commissions or expenditures may be permitted, such as talent agents' commissions, management commissions and actual touring expenses, but generally these deductions are capped somewhere between 10% - 25% of the gross fees.

Another model has begun to evolve at many independent labels and resembles a joint venture or economic partnership, whereby the label and artist share on an equal 50/50 basis in all net revenue created from all music and entertainment sources related to the artists' career. We'll discuss the structuring of these types of joint ventures in the chapter entitled New Creative Partnerships: the Joint Venture.

It remains to be determined whether this expansion of economic and administrative rights has actually resulted in significant financial gains for the labels, as most labels have no means to directly exploit these newly acquired rights and collection and enforcement of the rights is administratively burdensome and quite often impractical to pursue.

Chapter 2
What Happened To The Good Years?

The primary reasons that record companies began to look to their artists to create new and additional streams of income was the reality that illegal downloads removed billions of dollars from the income ledgers and sale of CDs have declined annually for the past fifteen years and have yet to be replaced by legal downloads.

Between 1999 and 2001 the peer-to-peer music file sharing website Napster was launched creating the beginning of the music industry's economic slide and eventual transition from physical to digital consumption. Many consumers (mostly teens and college students) now had an easily accessible platform for listening to music for free. Napster was co-founded by Shawn Fanning, John Fanning and Sean Parker (who went on to serve as founding President of Facebook, founder of Plaxo and an investor and Board of Directors member of Spotify) and quickly morphed into the world's leading P2P site. The site was eventually shut down by court order for copyright infringement but its technology opened the door to numerous successors. Companies such as Grokster, Gnutella, Freenet and Madster followed on the heels of Napster and one by one suffered similar fates.

Metallica and Dr. Dre are credited with starting the legal challenges against Napster when they discovered their music being shared for free without their permission on the site. Napster settled both of these lawsuits but a separate lawsuit commenced by the major labels ultimately sealed the coffin. Napster officially shuttered in July 2001 and filed for bankruptcy the following year. While Napster agreed to pay $36 million to the plaintiffs and various music creators, the loss in revenue to the labels, publishers, artists, songwriters, producers, musicians and singers was in the billions. From 2000 to 2009, 95% of music consumed was traded illegally (according to a study conducted by the International Federation of the Phonographic Industry - IFPI – 7).

The charts below demonstrate the impact of illegal downloads on legal CD and digital sales and the rise and fall of physical and digital sales between 2004 - 2013. This data was provided by the Recording Industry Association of America (RIAA).

U.S. Music Industry Shipment and Revenue Statistics

Year	Digital Singles	Digital Albums	SoundExchange Distributions (1)	CD	CD Singles	Total
2004	139.4 $138.0	4.6 $45.5	$6.9	767.0 $11,446.5	3.1 $15.0	958.0 $12,345.0
2005	366.9 $363.3	13.6 $135.7	$20.4	705.4 $10,520.2	2.8 $10.9	1,301.8 $12,289.9
2006	586.4 $580.6	27.6 $275.9	$32.8	619.7 $9,372.6	1.7 $7.7	1,588.5 $11,759.5
2007	819.4 $811.0	49.8 $497.4	$36.2	499.7 $7,452.3	2.6 $12.2	1,851.4 $10,651.0
2008	1,042.7 $1,032.2	63.6 $635.3	$100.0	368.4 $5,471.3	0.7 $3.5	1,919.7 $8,776.8
2009	1,124.4 $1,172.0	74.5 $744.3	$155.5	296.6 $4,318.8	0.9 $3.1	1,828.4 $7,831.1
2010	1,177.4 $1,336.4	85.8 $872.4	$249.2	253.0 $3,389.4	1.0 $2.9	1,739.6 $7,014.0
2011	1,332.3 $1,522.4	103.9 $1,070.8	$292.0	240.8 $3,100.7	1.3 $3.5	1,824.9 $7,135.6
2012	1,392.2 $1,623.6	116.7 $1,204.8	$462.0	198.2 $2,485.6	1.1 $3.2	1,803.3 $7,015.7
2013	1,328.9 $1,569.0	118.0 $1,233.5	$590.4	172.2 $2,123.5	0.6 $2.4	1,685.6 $6,996.1

Percentage of Shipments

	2005	2006	2007	2008	2009	2010	2011	2012	2013
Physical	91%	84%	75%	66%	60%	54%	49%	41%	36%
Digital	9%	16%	25%	34%	40%	46%	51%	59%	64%

©Recording Industry Association of America 2014

Footnotes:

(1) Estimated payments to performers and sound recording copyright owners for digital online music streaming services under statutory licenses.

(2) Units and dollar values are shown in millions of dollars.

The major labels failed to fully recognize the shifting trends in consumer music consumption and by the time they began to explore subscription models, the "cow was already out of the barn" and grazing in unfenced pastures. In this void of action, I-tunes rose from the ashes like a phoenix and Steve Jobs created what remains today as the world's leader in legal digital music purchase sites.

While legal digital music sales are continuing to increase annually and actually exceeded sales of physical CDs for the first time in 2011, it is unlikely that recorded music sales will ever return to their zenith when sales of 500,000 albums (gold certification in the United States) and 1,000,000 units (platinum certification in the United States) were commonplace. In 1999, the RIAA introduced the diamond award recognizing sales of 10,000,000 plus albums and bestowed this coveted plaque on 62 titles.

Several artists have topped the gold album certification pinnacle with scores of certifications including:

- The Beatles (45)
- Elvis Presley (81)
- Barbra Streisand (50)

However, the list of artists who have achieved gold album status over the past decade is extensive and includes, amongst others:

- George Strait (11)
- Jay-Z (10)
- Kenny Chesney (9)
- Bob Dylan (9)

- Dave Matthews Band (9)
- Kidz Bop Kids (9)
- Johnny Cash (8)
- Toby Keith (8)
- Grateful Dead (6)
- R. Kelly (6)
- Tony Bennett (6)
- Ludacris (6)
- Third Day (6)
- Rod Stewart (6)
- Snoop Dogg (6)
- Tim McGraw (6)
- Reba McEntire (6)
- Bruce Springsteen (6)
- Justin Bieber

Platinum Album recipients include:
- Elvis Presley (12)
- Jay-Z (11)
- Toby Keith (10)
- John Denver (9)
- The Rolling Stones (9)
- Dave Matthews Band (8)
- George Strait (8)
- The Eagles (7)
- Kenny Chesney (7)
- AC/DC (7)
- Justin Bieber (2)
- Johnny Cash (6)
- The Beatles (6)
- R. Kelly (6)
- Tim McGraw (6)
- Lil Wayne (1)

Diamond Award recipients include:
- The Beatles
- Garth Brooks
- The Eagles
- Led Zepplin
- Shania Twain

In 2013, the RIAA modified its gold and platinum award certification program to include digital streams of singles in the sales calculations.

Amongst the top sellers for 2013 were:
- Jay Z (2x Platinum)
- Justin Timberlake (Platinum)
- Robin Thicke (6x Platinum – single for "Blurred Lines")
- Lorde (4x Platinum – single)
- Katy Perry (4 x Platinum – single)
- Lorde (Gold – album)
- Daft Punk (3x Platinum – single)
- Fall Out Boys (3x Platinum – single)
- Ace Hood
- Tyler Farr
- Selena Gomez
- Ariana Grande
- Randy Houser
- Thomas Rhett
- Luke Bryan (Platinum – album)
- Hunter Hayes (Platinum – album)
- Blake Shelton (Platinum – album)

Diamond Certifications were awarded to:
- Justin Bieber (12x Platinum)
- Lady Gaga (10x Platinum)
- Eminem (11x Platinum)

A total of 167 digital songs were certified platinum in 2013; 258 singles were certified gold and 128 albums received certification.

As 2014 came to a close, 10 albums and 45 digital singles received gold and platinum certifications; a significant decline from 2013. Taylor Swift led the pack in 2014 followed by Miranda Lambert, Kanye West and Britt Nicole.

The above data demonstrates that the sale of recorded music is steadily declining (both physical and digital formats). Interestingly, sales of vinyl singles have remained relatively level over the past several years. Revenues from streaming music services continue to increase; contributing 21% to the 2013 total industry revenues, compared with 3% in 2007.

(The sales and certification data presented above was compiled by the Recording Industry Association of America.)

Chapter 3
The Rights Flow

Multiple Rights deals now involve multiple parties, from content creators (the artists) to the rights acquirers (labels, promoters, TV producers, manufacturers) to the rights exploiters (merchandising companies, book publishing companies, film studios, TV producers and networks and music publishers).

The chart below illustrates this intertwined music and rights community.

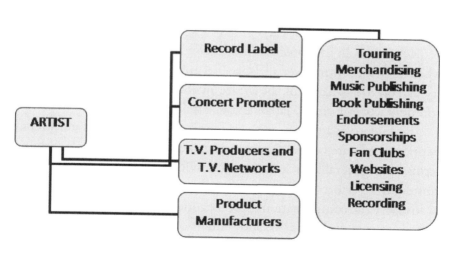

In addition to the more well known, highly publicized 360° deals, an expanding field of rights holders is beginning to emerge.

19 Entertainment, which owns the American Idol brand is one of the most successful producers of television programming who requires competitors to grant 360° rights in order to enter the competition. The American Idol contracts are virtually non-negotiable and the contestants have no leverage. With the success of the American Idol brand, which includes the seasonal TV series as well as concert tours featuring the top finalists, artists have a unique opportunity to perform weekly—during the season—for over 25 million viewers. That type of concentrated exposure has launched successful careers for scores of artists including Kelly Clarkson, Clay Aiken, Jennifer Hudson, Kellie Pickler, Chris Daughtry, Phillip Phillips, Ruben Studdard, Fantasia Barrino, Carrie Underwood, Taylor Hicks, Jordin Sparks, David Coal, Kris Allen, Lee DeWyze and Scotty McCreery.

American Idol has spawned numerous other television music competition shows including The Voice, the X-Factor, Making The Band and The Sing Off.

The Voice currently reigns in the United States as the most popular television music competition series. Originating in Holland in 2010 (created by Dutch T.V. Producer John de Mol), this show has now expanded its global footprint with local versions in approximately 52 countries, including the United States of America, China, France, Canada, Brazil, Australia, Germany, India, Israel, Italy, Mexico, Portugal, Russia, Thailand, Spain, Switzerland, the United Kingdom, Turkey and Vietnam.

The American Idol business model also includes artist management, which insures control over all aspects of an artist's entertainment industry career. The successful shows are mirrored around the world with counterparts in Europe, Japan and Australia.

The Talent/Contestant contracts for most of the televised music competition shows are basically non-negotiable for the substantive material terms; and generally include an exclusivity period covering all of the contestants' performing services in the entertainment, music and media industries. The compensation is pre-negotiated in the event a contestant records music, performs live and renders other related services.

As mentioned earlier, Live Nation has led the concert promoter community in signing superstar artists to multiple rights deals. Given Live Nation's predominance in the field of live entertainment, it is well suited to intersect all aspects of an artist's routing career, including merchandising. In order to effectively capitalize on and manage those newly acquired rights, Live Nation formed its Live Artists division in early 2007. The challenge faced by Live Nation is how to effectively manage the diverse array of rights which it has acquired in its deals with artists such as Jay-Z, Nickelback, Madonna and Shakira, which include recordings. In order to effectively administer and exploit certain of its rights, Live Nation has partnered with Universal Music Group to blend the strengths, corporate assets and leadership skills of the two companies to maximize revenues.

Other non-music industry companies are now entering into 360° deals with artists as well. Bacardi Rum landed a multiple rights deal with U.K. dance music act, Groove Armada, in March 2008, which includes recordings, touring, marketing and branding with liquor product tie-ins and music promotion. Their deal is described as an integrated marketing deal, under which Bacardi assumed responsibility for music production and promotion. The EDM act's music is cross promoted in Bacardi product ads, at sponsored events, through audio visual footage positioned on television.

Differing from the 10-year Live Nation deals, the deal between Bacardi and Groove Armada was a one year deal and the artist retained ownership of its masters and copyrights.

Another highly popularized non-traditional 360° pact was sealed between hit producer/artist, Timbaland, with Verizon in May 2008. Under this unique deal, Timbaland agreed to produce one song during each month of his deal to be released exclusively through Verizon's network. The songs acquired by Verizon from Timbaland were made available to Verizon subscribers through ringtone and ringback downloads. Timbaland also snagged a specially customized tour bus rigged for a recording studio. The following year, Verizon and Timbaland extended their deal to release exclusive content free for Blackberry Storm owners. As Verizon's official "Producer in Residence", Timbaland was able to expand his brand utilizing Verizon's market and ad muscle, while putting his music into the hands and ears of millions of new mobile listeners.

Chapter 4
Ancillary Rights Deal Models

Ancillary rights deals are being pursued through a variety of models. Many record labels include an ancillary rights provision within the body of their normal exclusive recording agreement. Several major labels and a few of the larger indies, however, have begun to present separate stand-alone contracts for their ancillary rights capture. Thus, an artist may receive an exclusive artist recording agreement, plus separate agreements for fan club, touring and merchandising rights. Under this scenario, each agreement may be distinct and unconnected to the others. Such an arrangement poses a new and different layer of concerns for the artist, which we'll address below.

Independent production companies who enter into an exclusive recording agreement with an artist are now, likewise, including an ancillary rights provision in their standard agreements. The range of participation varies widely and can run from five (5%) percent to fifty (50%) percent. Most major label deals generally include an ancillary rights share ranging from ten (10%) percent to twenty-five (25%) percent. The artist must be aware of the potentially overlapping (and double dip) into their 360° rights stream when signing with a production company, where the intention is to shop for a distribution deal. Specifically, the artist's negotiator must address the issues of what happens to the indie label or production company's ancillary rights share when a distribution or upstream deal is secured.

Ideally, the ancillary rights provision in the production agreement should provide that if and when the production company secures and enters into a distribution, recording, joint venture or custom label deal with a distributor, if the distribution agreement requires the artist to grant ancillary rights to the distributor, then the production company's share should decrease by the amount that the distributor is demanding from the artist.

The sample below provides an example of a fair and balanced ancillary rights provision which grants the production company a fifteen (15%) percent share in the ancillary income stream; ten (10%) percent for live engagements and reduces this participation to five (5%) percent, if and when a distribution agreement is obtained that includes a 360° clause in it.

Passive Income Participation.

(a) In the event the Distribution Agreement should contain any so-called "passive income provisions" which grant certain rights to the Distributor to receive a share of income, which you earn in connection with your activities in the entertainment industry (excluding records and music publishing), then you hereby grant to Company's Distributor, on a "pass through" basis as such necessary rights. Company shall be entitled to be paid and retain sums equivalent to an additional five (5%) percent of all such passive income streams as are paid to the Distributor, for Company's own account.

(b) Prior to the securing and execution of, and in the event the Distribution Agreement does not contain any so-called "passive income or 360 provisions", then the following shall apply:

(i) If you enter into an agreement with any third party with respect to any entertainment industry activity that would normally fall outside of the scope of this agreement (i.e., an agreement not related to Artist's recording services) (each, an "Ancillary Rights Agreement') (including, without limitation, any agreement for Artists acting services in motion pictures or television shows or services in connection with books, touring, endorsements, etc. [but specifically excluding music publishing]), you shall cause the applicable third party to pay Company directly an amount equal to ten percent (10%) for live engagements and fifteen (15%) percent for all other ancillary rights income streams of Ancillary Net Receipts in connection with any such Ancillary Rights Agreement.

(ii) Company shall have the same rights to audit your books and records (and to bring an action against you) in connection with any Ancillary Rights Agreement as you have to audit Company's Books and Records pursuant to paragraph 7(b) hereinbelow. As used herein, "Ancillary Net Receipts shall mean all royalties, one-time payments, or other compensation received by or credited to you or Artist in connection with any Ancillary Rights Agreement, less any actual and legitimate costs or expenses that you payor incur in connection with any such agreement (i.e., management fees, booking agent fees and legal fees)."

The most onerous arrangement for artists is the ancillary rights agreement which grants to the record label full and exclusive control over all of the artist's ancillary rights. Under this scenario the label acquires from the artist the right to control, license and administer an artist's

- touring rights
- film rights
- television rights
- literary rights
- merchandising rights
- theatrical rights
- and all other ancillary entertainment industry rights,
- sometimes including the publishing rights

Quite often there is no additional consideration or advances paid to the artist for giving up these rights and there is no guarantee of performance or definitive obligation placed on the record company to meaningfully and commercially exploit each rights stream. Thus, an artist can be left in a very vulnerable position of releasing control over his/her income opportunities and career and branding opportunities if the label is not equipped or sufficiently staffed to exploit such ancillary rights.

Therein lies the challenge. Due to decreasing music sales revenue, all of the major labels and larger independent labels have been forced to reduce overhead in order to remain financially solvent. This downsizing has resulted in numerous mergers, acquisitions and ownership changes, as well as reduced artist rosters and staffs, reduced recording, marketing and promotion budgets, lower artist advances and balancing the need to increase revenues—a ha!—the 360° ancillary rights model; designed to provide labels with a share of the artist's non-record sales revenue streams. Previously tabu, this expansion of rights has now become standard fare and has even begun to cross the entertainment industry sectors into television. Unfortunately, with reduced and downsized staffing, the remaining staffers are challenged to cover more areas of responsibility or continue their assigned duties with less support. Several labels have begun to enter into strategic alliances with non-affiliated companies who can provide the resources necessary to reasonably exploit the ancillary rights such as fan clubs and merchandising.

In most cases however, the bundle of ancillary rights granted to the record company go unexploited or remain a dormant right not pursued until the artist has achieved some level of commercial success. In reality, absent a chart topping hit record, followed by a nationwide or international tour, with a mix of merchandising and television appearances thrown in for good measure, an artist's ancillary rights income stream is modest, at best, and not worth the administrative time and manpower required to monitor and monetize the right. So, in many cases involving new and developing artists, the 360° clause is a dormant ticking volcano, awoken to eruption following a hit record.

Management and Administration of Rights

More complicated is the grant of exclusive control and administration of the artist's ancillary rights. Below is a sample of what such a provision looks like.

1. (a) Artist hereby grants to Company for the Ancillary Rights Term (as defined below), the exclusive right throughout the Territory to manage, control, exploit, administer and generally supervise the Artist's Ancillary Rights (as defined below). In connection therewith and to facilitate the exercise of Company duties hereunder, Artist grants to Company the right to use Artist's name, approved photographs and images, approved biography, trademark, autograph and marketing materials (the "Artist Elements"). Company shall have the right (and may license third parties) to exploit the Artist

Elements in connection with the exploitation of recordings, live engagements, concerts and tours, commercial endorsements and tie-ins, sponsorships, television programs, motion pictures, theatrical properties, books and other literary properties and merchandise (which shall include but not be limited to apparel, t-shirts, hats, posters, calendars, toys, key chains, cupholders, banners, jerseys, jackets and mugs).

(b) Company shall create designs and prototypes for the merchandise products for Artist's approval, not to be unreasonably withheld. Company shall exclusively own all designs, artwork, patterns, samples, covers and marketing materials created in connection with the Ancillary rights.

(c) The Ancillary Rights Term as used herein shall be defined as the Term (of this Agreement) plus an additional nine (9) months after the expiration of the Term. During the Ancillary Rights Term, Company shall have the right to license, sublicense and grant others any of the rights conveyed to Company herein. Company shall also take such actions as it deems appropriate to protect the intellectual property and proprietary rights connected to the Artist Elements.

(d) Artist agrees to cooperate with Company as and when and where requested for the purpose of creating the merchandise products, conducting media interviews, making personal appearances, reviewing designs and samples for approval, protecting the rights, making recordings, taking photographs and interacting with fans (i.e. meet and greets), subject to Artist's prior professional commitments and at Company's expense.

(e) "Artist's Ancillary Rights" as that term is used herein shall be defined as live engagements, literary, motion picture, television, videos, merchandising, fan clubs, online websites, radio, games, theatrical properties, cartoons, magazines and all non-music entertainment industry activities.

2. (a) Company shall account to and pay to Artist the following shares of net receipts earned and collected by it:
    (i) live engagements   :   85%
    (ii) books, magazines and literary properties   :   80%
    (iii) film, television and radio   :   75%

(iv) merchandise	:	75%
(v) fan clubs and online sites	:	75%
(vi) theatrical properties	:	80%
(vii) games	:	75%
(viii) all other properties	:	75%

(b) Company shall render accountings to Artist with respect to the Artist Ancillary Rights on a quarterly basis, within sixty (60) days after March 31st, June 30th, September 30th and December 31st. Accounting statements shall be accompanied by payment of the Artist's share of ancillary net receipts, if any.

(c) Company shall not cross-collateralize Artist's Ancillary Rights net receipts with Artist's record royalty account.

(d) the term "net receipts" as used in this paragraph "2" shall be defined as Ancillary Rights gross receipts less any and all actual costs and expenditures incurred in connection with the creation and exploitation of the Artist Ancillary Rights; including but not limited to manufacturing, distribution, licensing, commissions, taxes, design fees, legal and accounting fees, marketing and promotion costs and travel costs, but excluding Company's normal overhead.

3. Artist hereby acknowledges that Company's exercise of the Artist's Ancillary Rights hereunder shall not be deemed to be a partnership, joint venture or artist personal management relationship; and shall not create a fiduciary relationship between the parties. Artist hereby acknowledges that Company is not an employment or theatrical agency and has made no promises to solicit or secure employment. Artist agrees to separately engage a personal manager and talent agent to handle all such matters on behalf of Artist as are customarily handled by personal managers and talent agents."

This provision must be taken more seriously than the so-called "passive income participation" model because under this scenario, the artist effectively gives up control over all or substantially all of his/her music and entertainment industry rights and revenue streams. Failure to adhere to the contract will result in a material breach of the agreement, which could lead to other penalties, suspension of the running of the term, termination of the agreement and possible legal proceedings. Generally, a new unproven artist will not have sufficient leverage to push back against a broad reaching grant such as this, but at a minimum, the artist's negotiator should suggest several caveats (which we will discuss in detail in a subsequent chapter) to lessen the bite.

Legal Precedent

While the United States Courts have yet to issue a ruling on the enforceability of such exclusive rights management provisions or contracts in the music sector, the courts in the United Kingdom have already addressed similar issues in favor of the artist.

In a case heard before the English courts in 1991, Silvertone Records vs. Montfield, known as the Stone Roses case, the Court effectively ruled that music contracts which extract exclusive rights and obligations from an artist without any obligation on the company to perform, was an unreasonable restraint of trade. The Stone Roses signed a recording and publishing agreement with Zomba Productions Limited (later assigned to Silvertone Records) in 1988. The recording and publishing agreements were a joint package and could not be separated (as per the label's demands). By 1990, the group was disgruntled and litigation ensued. In 1991, the Court determined that the recording contract did not obligate the Company to any affirmative obligations such as releasing or distributing records, but required the artist to exclusively record for the label with ownership of the masters vesting in perpetuity in the label. A re-recording restriction also prohibited the group from re-recording any masters which they had recorded for the label. The Court found both contracts to be an unreasonable restraint of trade and held in favor of the artist in letting them out of the deals. The pivoting factor in this case was the demand for certain rights by the record company without any corresponding obligation to exploit them, thus sterilizing the artist's career.

The standard 360° contract or clause does not obligate the record company to exploit the rights granted and since there are usually no additional advances paid for these rights, there is no legal consideration exchanged. Thus, the artist is left at a disadvantage unless they have some leverage or an experienced negotiator to claw back some of the rights or reduce the label share of receipts. The following chapter discusses negotiation strategies.

The Joint Venture

Another model which is evolving into a more frequent structure is the joint venture. Quite a few independent labels and production companies have adopted this "partnership" concept and model, and it has become their standard record deal format. Under the joint venture or "JV" template, the label and artist become partners with respect to the artist's career. Generally, this involves formation of a limited liability company or a corporation wherein the equity is owned equally or some other close variable like 55/45, 60/40, etc. The operating agreement or shareholders agreement which governs the parties' rights and obligations specifies that the artist's recording, performing, touring, merchandising, ancillary and often publishing rights will be granted exclusively to the JV entity during the term of the agreement. It will also provide that the label will fund the recordings, release, market and promote the music and provide administrative back-up services. Those services can include issuing third party licenses, collecting and disbursing revenue, publishing administration, tour support and tour management. Essentially, the artist assumes the role of the creative talent and the label assumes the role of financier, marketing and promotion entity, administrator and accounting. Under an equitable agreement, the copyrights in the masters—or the sound recordings—will be owned by the JV, which gives the Artist equity ownership in their masters.

The JV model provides a hybrid, blending elements of the traditional exclusive artist recording agreement, the passive income participation model, with the exclusive control/administration model with a traditional general partnership, albeit without the legal liabilities of a standard partnership. It is important for the artist's negotiator to provide checks and balances as well as comprehensive lists of rights, responsibilities, obligations, profits distribution, exit rights, post term rights, dispute procedures and in the case of smaller indie labels or production companies, a "keyman" clause tied to the owner or CEO.

See Appendix 1 for a sample of a joint venture 360 agreement.

Chapter 5
Deconstructing The Deal— Negotiating Points

Let's examine and dissect the material components of the typical ancillary rights agreement and explore key negotiating points to balance out the rights and maintain a reasonable amount of control and income flow for the artist. The concepts below can be utilized by artists at varying levels of career status; from new and developing, to established.

I.   The Label Share
A.   Live Engagements.

The basic premise of the 360° deal is that the record company now shares in the income streams created by their artists' non-record activities in the entertainment industry. As mentioned previously, label shares can range from five (5%) to fifty (50%) percent depending on the structure of the deal and the revenue source. Most labels will agree to a modest concession, which reduces their share for live appearances and touring. This concession is granted primarily because the artist has layers of additional expenditures, which are associated with concerts that are absent from the other ancillary areas such as fan clubs, merchandising, television, literary and motion pictures.

While many deals may provide for a label share ranging between ten (10%) percent to twenty five (25%) percent for live engagements, a much fairer range is ten (10%) percent to fifteen (15%) percent and there are many considerations which go into this calculation. For example, should the label share be calculated on the basis of gross or net touring receipts? For the artist, net is always best or in the alternative, a significantly adjusted gross. Here are some of the practical concerns related to the artist's live engagement income and expenditures and the applicable label share calculation.

Let's use a typical engagement sheet to demonstrate.

Income:
    A. Gross Talent Fee: $10,000
Expenses:
    B. Commissions:
        (i) Talent Agent (10%) $1,000
        (ii) Manager (20%) $2,000
        (iii) Business Manager/CPA (5%) $ 500
    C. Salaries:*
        (i) Road Manager $ 500
        (ii) Back-Up Singers (3) $ 750
        (iii) Dancers (2) $ 500
        (iv) Band (5) $1,250
        (v) Sound Engineer $ 350
        (vi) Per Diems (@ $50 each) $ 600
    D. Travel:**
        (i) Hotel (1 night x 8 rooms)   <u>$1,200</u>

Total Expenses: $8,650

NET TO ARTIST BEFORE LABEL SHARE <u>**$1,350**</u>
    Less a 10% label share $1,000
FINAL NET TO ARTIST   **$ 350**

*/estimates
**/assuming an airline ticket and ground transportation is a contribution by the promoter

Many new artists are not able to command per show fees of $10,000 and, therefore, either perform to tracks, if appropriate, or if live, they reduce their band and crew size and salaries to remain financially solvent.

So, let's look at comparable calculations for a reasonably established artist, at a higher fee level.

Income:
A.	Gross Talent Fee:	$25,000

Expenses:
B.	Commissions:		
	(i) Talent Agent (10%)		$2,500
	(ii) Manager (20%)		$5,000
	(iii) Business Manager/CPA (5%)		$1,250
C.	Salaries:*		
	(i) Road Manager		$ 750
	(ii) Back-Up Singers (3)		$1,050
	(iii) Dancers (2)		$ 700
	(iv) Band (5)		$1,750
	(v) Sound Engineers (2)		$1,000
	(vi) Per Diems (@ $50 each)		$ 600
D.	Travel:**		
	(i) Hotel (1 suite)		$ 300
	(ii) Hotel (1 single)		$ 250
	(iii) Hotel (6 doubles)		$ 900

Total Expenses:	$16,050

NET TO ARTIST BEFORE LABEL SHARE	**$8,950**
Less a 10% label share	$2,500
FINAL NET TO ARTIST	**$6,450**

Please note that the above calculations do not include several additional typical touring expenses which also reduce the artist's net share such as hotel gratuities, artist's personal hotel incidentals, taxes, excess airline baggage fees, etc.

As you see, at a low end label share of ten (10%) percent, for the new and developing artist, the label share, the manager's commission and the talent agent's commission can each exceed the net share that the artist takes home from a gig. For the mid-level and more established artist as portrayed in our model above, the net artist share, assuming a low ten (10%) percent label share can be in the range of twenty-five (25%) percent of the gross fee for the show.

Therefore, it is incumbent upon the artist's negotiator to not only REDUCE the label share to reasonable ranges (i.e. 5%—10%) but also permit certain deductions prior to the calculation of the label share, such as the talent agency and management commissions. Quite a few labels now permit reasonable commission and/or expense deductions prior to calculating their share; however, they will usually insist on a cap on such deductions of approximately twenty (20%) percent to twenty five (25%) percent. Another negotiating point to raise in the label share entitlement is to stipulate that the label share will not apply to any engagements below a minimum threshold; i.e. Five Thousand ($5,000) or Ten Thousand ($10,000) Dollars. Thus, for developing or new artists, the label will waive its income participation until such time as the artist is earning so-called "real money".

In most cases, the administrative time and manpower resources required for a label to enforce its live engagement ancillary rights is justified only when the artist is at a significant earnings level and is touring regularly. Otherwise, the label is faced with the task of policing the touring activities for each artist on a show-by-show basis. With many developing artists doing their own direct bookings or utilizing smaller independent agents, monitoring one-offs with a reduced staff and limited access to information is impractical. The process is further complicated by the fact that there is no uniform system in place for labels to monitor their artist's live performances with any sort of certainty, let alone determine how much an artist makes for each engagement. Double sets of contracts routinely exist in the live performance business for a variety of reasons; most often to underreport fees. Thus, monetizing a label's touring ancillary rights can become a veritable cat and mouse game.

B.   Merchandising.

Label shares for merchandising rights generally range between fifteen (10%) percent to twenty five (25%) percent and are calculated on either gross receipts or a slightly adjusted gross receipts formula. In the negotiation process, an artist should seek to have broker's commissions, cost of goods and fixed sales/licensing expenditures taken off the top, prior to calculating the label share. Merchandising rights are typically licensed to third party merchandising companies such as Bravado, Signatures Network, Revolve Merchandise, BandMerch and others who work with labels or directly with artists to design, manufacture and sell a wide array of products. For the most part, record companies are not in the merchandising or branding business, hence, a label's role in an artist's merchandising exploitation will be passive or at best, middle party broker between artist and merchandiser.

Let's look at the label/artist share calculations for this rights stream. Assuming a twenty five (25%) percent label share, the numbers would look like this:

Income:

A.	Gross Receipts Payable By Merchandiser	$10,000

Expenses:

B.	Commissions:	
	(i) Manager's Commission (20%)	$2,000
	(ii) Business Manager/CPA (5%)	$1,000
	(iii) Label Share (25%)	<u>$2,500</u>

NET ARTIST SHARE   **$4,500**

Under this scenario, the artist will realize a net share equivalent to forty five (45%) percent of the merchandising royalties. After taxes, this sum will be reduced by another thirty (30%) percent to thirty five (35%) percent, leaving about Three Thousand ($3,000) Dollars, net to the artist.

So what appears on first blush to be a decent merchandising check is quickly reduced to a fraction of its original amount.

Another common merchandising arrangement entails the grant of exclusive merchandising rights to the label during the term of the recording agreement. Such a provision vests full control of the merchandising activities in the label with the artist's involvement limited to product approval. Below is a sample merchandising clause contained in many recording agreements.

"Artist hereby grants to Company the exclusive right during the Term and for the Territory, to use the Artist's approved likeness, name, approved images, approved pictures, facsimile signature and approved biographical materials (the "Materials") either alone or together with such other elements as Company, in its sole discretion, may elect to utilize in connection with the sale, design, development, licensing, promotion, marketing, advertising or other exploitation of any so-called merchandise, which shall include but not be limited to tie-ins, concert tour merchandising, retail merchandising, bounce-back merchandising, fan clubs and social media. The merchandising uses shall include but not be limited to apparel, hats, posters, flyers, buttons, housewares, automobiles, fragrances, alcoholic beverages, soft drinks and food.

Company shall accrue to Artist's account a royalty equivalent to fifty (50%) percent of all of Company's net merchandising receipts actually paid to Company in connection with the merchandising uses. The term "net merchandising receipts" shall be defined as the gross merchandising related revenues actually paid to Company by its licensees less any and all costs and expenditures incurred by Company in connection therewith, including but not limited to design and development costs, costs of sales, commissions, legal fees, accounting fees, marketing and promotion costs, shipping and insurance costs, and taxes.

Company shall render accountings to artist with respect to merchandising at the same times and subject to the same terms as it renders royalty accountings to artist hereunder. Royalties accruing to artist for merchandising shall not be applied in recoupment of other advances made and recoupable against artist's royalties hereunder."

Notwithstanding the foregoing, in the event Company should exploit the merchandising rights directly (as opposed to through a third party merchandising company), then Company will accrue to artist's account the following royalties:

"Company will accrue to your account the following royalties (the "Artist Merchandise Share") with respect to merchandising exploitations under this Agreement:

1. (i) With respect to sales by Company, Company will account to you for a royalty calculated on the consumer price of twenty-five (25%) percent with respect to standard weight T-shirts; twenty-five (25%) with respect to standard sweatshirts, long-sleeve T-shirts and mid-level T-shirts; twenty (20%) percent with respect to girls' and juniors' T-shirts and tank tops and with respect to track jackets, skirts, shorts, premium t-shirts and premium sweatshirts; and twenty (20%) percent with respect to hats, pins, accessories and all other categories.

(ii) With respect to sales through retail stores, Company will account to you for a royalty calculated on the wholesale price of twenty-five (25%) percent with respect to standard weight T-shirts and standard sweatshirts and eighteen (18%) percent with respect to long-sleeve T-shirts, mid-level T-shirts, girls' and juniors' T-shirts and tank tops, track jackets, skirts, shorts, premium T-shirts and sweatshirts and hat, pins, accessories and all other categories.

(iii) With respect to sales through third party licensees, Company will account to you for a royalty of seventy-five (75%) percent of our Net Merchandise Receipts.

(iv) Notwithstanding anything to the contrary herein, with respect to sales of merchandise products by us or our affiliates outside of the United States, the royalty will be seventy (70%) percent of the otherwise applicable rate set forth above, and with respect to third party licenses related to products outside of the United States, Artist will receive sixty-five (65%) percent of the Net Merchandise Receipts.

(v) A used in this section: "consumer price" means the selling price paid by the consumer, less applicable sales taxes, value-added tax or its equivalent, returns or credits on returns; "wholesale price" means the net wholesale price received by us (i.e. net of any allowances, rebates or other discounts); and "Net Merchandise Receipts" means all monies received by us in the United States from the applicable sale of products, less applicable sales taxes, value-added tax or its equivalent, import duties, credit card service fees, costs of freight, insurance and returns.

2. All costs paid or incurred by us in connection with the creation of any materials or designs, including without limitation all merchandise rights acquisition costs and fifty (50%) percent of all other artwork costs, will be deemed Advances recoupable from royalties credited to you under this Agreement.

3. Company will account to you in respect of the Artist merchandise share at the same times and pursuant to the same terms, to the extent applicable, as set forth in this Agreement for record royalties. Notwithstanding anything to the contrary contained herein, Company will maintain a separate account with respect to the artist merchandise share, which account will not be cross-collateralized with any other account that Company maintain with respect to other royalties payable to you hereunder."

2. Pre-Conditions To Label Rights
A. Sales and Release Thresholds

A plausible argument can be made by an artist that a label's ancillary rights and income participation should be subject to some sort of performance by the label. In a true partnership, both parties are expected to make meaningful contributions to the venture; whether financing, services or goods or some combination of the various elements. In a contractual recording relationship, the artist naturally brings the creative talent, which can include singing, songwriting, production, performing and playing an instrument; while the label will bring financing, marketing, promotion and distribution to the table. What happens though when an artist signs a record deal which only obligates the label to initially release one or two singles with the album production and release, relying predominantly on the success of the singles? Or what about a situation where an album commitment is made out of the box, but recording that album takes a year or more? Or what about instances where the label records and releases the first album, but it turns out to be a commercial flop and sells less than 50,000 units?

The customary ancillary rights agreement or clause within the recording agreement provides that the label's ancillary rights and income entitlement commence upon the execution of the contract. Therefore, the record company will begin to have the right to collect its share of the artist's non-record income from day one of the contract without any regard to whether the label has spent any money on the artist, has released any product, has promoted and marketed the releases, has achieved any commercial success with the artist or has made any contributions to assist the artist in exploiting his/her non-record rights. In these cases, most would call this a free or unearned ride. When the label pays execution and recording advances, releases and aggressively promotes the artist's records and provides other resources and support to help brand an artist, the ancillary rights participation from day one of the recording contract is more reasonable.

One negotiating position to help balance out the competing label/ artist interests is to condition the commencement of the label's ancillary income flow upon achieving a specific sales threshold. This condition supports the label's argument that it has made a significant and meaningful contribution to the branding and commercial success of the Artist. As an example, the artist can request a reasonable benchmark of new album sales to trigger the label's rights. Below is a sample of a sales threshold provision:

"The Term of the Company's income participation rights shall commence upon the execution of this Agreement and shall continue for a period of time which is coterminous with the Term of the Exclusive Recording Agreement hereof. Company's right to receive the so-called label share, as described above, shall only apply if an album released hereunder achieves net U.S. sales (of full priced albums) of 100,000 units. Company shall have the right to receive its label share by sending artist written notice of its election within sixty (60) days after the sales threshold is met (the "effective date"). If Company exercises its right, as described above, then Company shall be entitled to be paid its label share prospectively with respect to all covered income streams. For the purpose of clarification, Company shall not be entitled to be paid with respect to income and revenue which was earned and accrued, but was not yet paid to artist prior to the effective date. Once Company has exercised its option to receive the label share, it shall continue to be entitled to receive such revenue for the remainder of the Term of this Agreement."

Another possible condition or threshold is to require the release of the album in key foreign territories in order for the label to have a right to share in the non-record revenue generated by the artist in that particular country. For clarification, the ancillary rights provisions grant worldwide 360° rights to the label. However, just because the label has exclusive worldwide recording rights does not mean that product will be released outside of the United States. Therefore, it's possible that a record company could release an album on an artist in say, the United States, Canada and the U.K. but nowhere else (except online) with an active in market promotion limited to the countries of actual (physical) release. Now add into the mix an active touring artist who performs in numerous foreign countries such as the U.K., Germany, Italy, Holland, Australia, Japan, Brazil, Mexico and Canada. Well, the label will have the right to share in the touring revenue earned in all of these foreign markets, even though they may not have released or promoted the artist's albums in many of those markets. Availability of product online through i-tunes worldwide does not mean that any marketing and promotion money is being spent in a particular market.

B. Exclusions From Covered Activities

Quite often an artist may already have an established career or income stream in another sector of the entertainment industry such as acting, modeling or (book) writing. In cases such as these, the label cannot say that their investment in the artist's music career and expanding brand was responsible for their entry or success in the field in which activity was pre-existing.

Whenever an artist can clearly demonstrate that, prior to the execution of the recording agreement, they were performing in stage plays, had roles in television shows or motion pictures, had one or more books published or have existing endorsements or sponsors, they can negotiate for the exclusion from the 360° capture of these fields of endeavor. However, keep in mind that if the non-record activities were very basic or developmental (i.e. local community theater or one self-published, not so successful book or an extra role in the film or television show), then there will be little to no leverage to exclude these areas of non-record activity from the 360° deal. When there is leverage and justification to exclude a rights stream, the following language can be inserted:

"Notwithstanding anything to the contrary set forth herein, Company shall have no right to receive the "label share" with respect to any revenue earned by the Artist during the Term hereof in connection with his/her activities in the field of _____."

C. Minimum Income Thresholds

Each non-record activity has its own unique and separate income stream. As discussed earlier, live engagements and touring has layers of expenses and commissions, which must be paid from the gross talent fee prior to calculating the artist's net income per show; therefore, it is incumbent upon the artist to carve out as many expenses as possible before calculating and paying the label share. Another carve out is to exclude from label participation any engagements which pay the artist less than a stipulated gross fee; i.e. Five Thousand ($5,000) Dollars. This will insure that a new or developing artist will not be stifled (as in our prior example) by excessive fees and commissions when they are being paid minimal amounts. The following language is an example of such an exclusion:

> "Notwithstanding anything to the contrary set forth herein, Company shall have no right to receive the "label share" with respect to live engagements, individual "one off" shows" or other personal appearances in which the Artist is paid gross income less than \$_____. Such calculations shall be on a case-by-case basis and shall not be cumulative."

D. Music Publishing

More frequently, record companies (majors and indies alike) are beginning to include music publishing within the scope of covered 360° activities and income streams. Some deals call for an outright assignment of a share of the artist's copyright interest in each song written by the artist during the Term of the recording agreement. This is nothing less than a traditional co-publishing arrangement, simply couched under the cloak of ancillary rights. Other deals call for a passive income participation in the artist's publishing revenue (publisher and sometimes writer shares). Generally, when the music publishing income stream is included in the ancillary rights clause or contract, it will not include administration rights. If the publishing rights grant covers only an income share and not a copyright conveyance, then the artist should retain exclusive administrative rights. Otherwise, the subsequent closing of a co-publishing or administration deal with a music publisher will be complicated by the prior grants to the record company of overlapping and possibly conflicting rights. As a general rule of thumb, an artist should utilize whatever leverage they have to exclude music publishing rights and income from the non-record rights provisions.

E. Advances

Very few recording contracts provide for additional advances to be paid to the artist for the grant of non-record rights. Nonetheless, if you never ask, you can't expect to receive. Several years ago, when 360° clauses were first introduced, several major labels routinely included advances or participation fees payable to the artist in their deals. This practice has quickly faded away. There are many variations and nuances for including advances in the ancillary rights provision.

First, the artist should request a non-recoupable, non-returnable execution fee as a general payment (consideration) for the non-record rights grant. Such a payment accomplishes a few goals. It compensates the artist for giving up an income stream in their non-record activities for what could be a 5-8 year period. It simultaneously puts "skin in the game" for the label and ideally gives the record company extra incentive to support and assist in the branding of their artist. The larger the brand, the greater the financial return.

Typically, if an advance is paid, it is more likely than not that the advance will be recoupable and that's where an artist needs to focus on exactly which royalty streams will be subject to recoupment of the ancillary rights advance. There are several possible streams:

(i)   record royalties
(ii) mechanical royalties (a no-no)
(iii) merchandising royalties
(iv) ancillary rights income

More often than not, the record company will state in the negotiations that the general artist or "all inclusive fund" advances are intended to include all rights—recording as well as non-record rights. Where advances are agreed upon, the advances for non-record rights should be paid out on an album-by-album basis, and not simply a single one time advance on execution or completion of the first album. The reason for this is simple, each album cycle will typically last for twelve (12) to eighteen (18) months, which is the period of time that runs from the commencement of recording until the normal sales cycle for the album (9-12 months after its initial release). Just like a record label pays an advance to its artist for each album recorded, the ancillary rights advances should be no different.

The timing for payment of the advance must also be considered and negotiated. The three most likely trigger events are the commencement of recording, the completion of recording and delivery or upon the initial release of the album. From the artist's perspective, the sooner the better, while the label's position will likely be directly opposite.

Without a doubt, an artist should resist having any ancillary rights advances cross-collateralized or recouped from record or publishing income streams. There is a separate and distinct bundle of rights and has no relationship to direct expenses being made by the label such as recording costs. Also, most often, the label is not required to provide any services to secure non-record income earning opportunities or to monetize the rights for the artist; which is why it is often referred to as a passive income participation. Under no circumstances should an ancillary rights advance be unconditionally returnable, like a loan. Below is a sample of an ancillary rights advance clause.

F. New Music Related Income Streams

SoundExchange is an independent digital performance rights organization which was created as a result of the Digital Millennium Copyright Act of 1998 and the Digital Performance Right in Sound Recordings Act of 1995. SoundExchange offers free membership to artists (main/feature artists) and sound recording copyright owners (SRCO's or more commonly known as record labels and independent production companies).

By legislation and U.S. Copyright Office policy, SoundExchange collects royalties from non-interactive digital music streaming services such as Sirius/XM Satellite, Pandora, Music Choice, Spotify and thousands of webcasters, large and small. In 2014, Sound Exchange collected approximately $772 Million in royalties worldwide and distributed over $773 Million in payments to its members (with a lower administration rate than other performing rights organizations).

Similar to the music publishing performing rights organizations which allocate and pay in equal shares, royalties to their songwriter and publisher members, SoundExchange royalties are allocated: fifty (50%) percent to the feature artists (with 5% of this amount going to background vocalists and musicians via AFofM and SAG/AFTRA); and fifty (50%) percent to the SRCO.

The payments are clearly and evenly allocated amongst the content creator/artists and the record label or SR copyright owner (which in many cases is also the indie artist/label owner). Over 90,000 artists and over 28,000 SRCO's have registered with SoundExchange and over $2 Billion in royalties have been distributed since the organization's launch.

Recently, many labels have sought to enter into new contractual arrangements with their recording artists which grant the label the right to collect the artist's share of SoundExchange royalties and apply it against the artist's unrecouped royalty balance (incurred from advances, recording, promotion and other recoupable advances). The artist community has and continues to fight against this encroachment into what remains a definitive unencumbered revenue source. In some cases, language is included in artist/label joint venture agreements which throws all artist generated revenue into one pot (including music sales, publishing, touring, merchandising, endorsements, media and SoundExchange). All joint venture expenses are then recouped from the gross revenues and the resulting net profit (if any) is allocated between the artist and label in accordance with percentage shares to be negotiated (i.e. 50/50).

With music sales revenues on the decline (both physical and digital), artists have a steadily decreasing pool of unencumbered revenue streams. Record royalty payments are made only after the record label recoups its recording costs, in pocket artist advances, all or a portion of its marketing and promotion costs, tour support and miscellaneous designated recoupable expenses. With declining music sales, very few recording artists ever receive a meaningful record royalty check from their label.

Most recording artists are also songwriters; and therefore, receive music publishing income as a result of their copyright and songwriter interests. The performing rights organizations such as ASCAP, BMI and SESAC in the United States pay songwriters and music publishers separately (50/50). Thus, as an artist songwriter, unless you have an unrecouped advance outstanding, you will receive quarterly performing rights royalty statements and payments.

Another primary source of revenue for recording artists is live appearance fees for concerts, club performances, "walk throughs" and guest appearances at events. Depending upon the contract terms for the particular engagement, the payment to the artist can be either net of all costs or gross with certain expenses to be borne by the Artist from the gross fee. The ancillary rights agreements will grant to the record label a share (i.e.: 10% - 25%) of the artist's fee from these endeavors. It is incumbent upon the artist and their representatives to insure that the label share is calculated as close to the artist's actual in-pocket net as possible, but not to exceed ten (10%) percent of the gross.

G. Miscellaneous Ancillary Revenue Streams

The transitional 360/Ancillary Rights agreements will also grant to the record company the right to share in revenues earned, during the Term by the Artist from:

(i)   literary rights
(ii) film and TV rights
(iii) fan clubs

Typically, the label share initially requested for these revenue streams is 20% - 25%. Almost always, the label has very little, if any, involvement in directly generating the income earned by its artists in these areas; however, the rationale is that the label expended significant sums of money in promoting the artist, creating the artist's "brand" and helping to monetize a new career; and thus, should share in the fruits of its investment and labor, similar to the personal manager.

On a case-by-case basis, some labels will agree to permit its artist to first deduct certain direct expenses related to these streams prior to calculating the label share, such as:

(i)   talent or literary agent commissions
(ii) legal fees incurred to negotiate the contract
(iii) management commissions
(iv) direct and necessary expenses incurred to perform the agreement.

H. The Term

The "Term" is the period of time during which the record company will have the right to participate in the ancillary revenue streams and collect its share. Be mindful of the language.

In many cases, the Term may be defined as the term of the artist recording agreement plus an additional period of time after the expiration of the Term (i.e. another 6-12 months, post-Term). Below is such an example:

"Artist will pay to Label twenty five (25%) percent of all gross ancillary (non-record) revenues without any deductions or offsets earned and payable to Artist (or Artist's designee) during the Term hereof and twelve (12) months thereafter pursuant to any agreements or engagements entered into by the Artist during the Term, in connection with the following services rendered by Artist: touring and all live performances, acting, literary, film and television roles, merchandising, sponsorships, clothing lines, jewelry, fragrances, beverages (alcohol and non-alcohol), tobacco products, games, broadcasting and fan clubs."

The primary issue for an artist when the ancillary rights Term extends past the expiration or termination of the recording agreement is that there may be a period of time during which the artist is potentially liable to pay a share of their revenue to two different labels. By way of example, if an artist negotiates with a new label for a deal which commences when the artist's current record deal expires, the artist must carve out an initial start date for the new label ancillary rights share so that the new label rights commence upon the expiration of the prior label's rights. Otherwise, the artist could be contractually obligated to pay ancillary rights label shares simultaneously to the old and the new label; possible equaling 25% - 50% in the aggregate.

Another negotiating option would be to reduce the "post-Term" ancillary label share to a fraction of the regular ("Term") share. By way of example, if the label has an ancillary revenue stream share of fifteen (15%) percent during the Term and demands a limited period post-Term share, then the artist should seek to reduce the post-Term (or "sunset") share to possibly ten (10%) percent or seven and one half (7.5%) percent; thereby leaving more revenue available for negotiating the new record deal.

I. Accounting (How Does The Label Collect):

How do the record labels actually collect their share of ancillary revenues? There are a few standard models.

A. Direct Third Party Payments.

Most ancillary rights agreements include an accounting provision which calls for the artist to authorize and direct (through a letter of direction) each third party licensee/payor to render accountings and remit payments directly to the label. Under this structure, an artist will include in their third party (ancillary) deal a provision which directs the payor to remit directly to the label, the "label share" of applicable fees, advances and royalties, simultaneous with the third party's remittance of accounting statements and payments to the artist. Below is a sample of the language which effectuates this arrangement.

"You will irrevocably direct and cause each person from which you or any person receiving revenues on your behalf receive Ancillary Income ("Third Party"), to account directly to Label for Label's share of such Ancillary Income at the same times and subject to the same accounting terms, as apply to accountings, to you, but no less frequently than semi-annually. You shall use your best efforts to cause all agreements with Third Parties (each, an "Ancillary Income Agreement") to provide that Label shall have the right to examine each Third Party's books and records with respect to Ancillary Income, subject to the same terms and limitations as apply to accountings to you. Without limiting the foregoing, (i) you will use your best efforts to cause all Ancillary Income Agreements to provide that the Third Party concerned will account directly to Label for its share of Ancillary Income and that Label shall have such right to examine such books and records, and (ii) Label shall have the right to examine your books and records (upon reasonable notice to you, at your office where the records concerned are kept, provided at Label's request, you will make all such records available, not more frequently than once per twelve (12) month period). You will notify Label upon conclusion of each Ancillary Income Agreement if you have not obtained such direct accounting and audit rights for the Label. Nothing in any Ancillary Income Agreement will relieve you of your obligation to make such payments to Label if not paid to Label by the applicable Third Party within fifteen (15) days after the rendering of each accounting to you, which includes such Ancillary Income concerned or within fifteen (15) days after receipt by you, or on your behalf, of such Ancillary Income if for any reason not included in an accounting, in each instance; and you will be liable to Label for all such payments not made to Label as required hereunder."

In most cases, companies with accounting obligations are reluctant to treat passive royalty participants as third party beneficiaries with full audit rights. Since there is no direct contractual privity between the passive royalty recipient (i.e. the "Label") and the Third Party, the latter has no incentive to further open their books and records to a non-party, along with the cost, administrative burden and staffing demands created by an audit. Thus, an artist should seek to eliminate such a direct audit rights clause, or at most, agree to use "reasonable (not best)" efforts to obtain such rights from the Third Party for the benefit of the Label.

B. Accounting From Artist.

Another method used by certain labels provides that the artist will render periodic accountings and remit payments to the label for its share of all covered ancillary receipts. This structure places the administrative burden directly and solely on the artist to (1) keep good books and records of all ancillary revenue deals and transactions, (2) prepare periodic accounting statements (typically quarterly or semi-annually), and (3) set aside in a segregated reserve account the label share of ancillary receipts so that the funds are readily available when payments are due. Without financial discipline and business management back-up, most artists will falter on point #3 and fail to set aside a reserve account; not to be comingled with their general operating account. Below is a sample of the language typically used to effectuate this type of arrangement.

"Artist shall account for and pay to Label twenty (20%) percent of Artist's Net Ancillary Revenues (as that term is defined below) promptly following the close of each calendar quarter during the Term of this Agreement (but in no event later than thirty (30) days after the close of each such quarterly period) and continuing for a period of twelve (12) months after the expiration of the Term with respect to all Ancillary contracts entered into during the Term.

The term "Net Ancillary Revenues" shall be defined as all gross revenues, including but not limited to advances, fees, royalties, cash gifts and other remuneration paid to Artist and/or to artist's affiliates, managers, representatives, accountants, attorneys, agents, employees, successors and assigns, in connection with Artist's services in all non-record entertainment areas, including film, television, theatrical, live touring and performances, endorsements, merchandising, sponsorships, clothing lines, jewelry, beverages and literary, but excluding music publishing, less only the following:

Actual talent and/or literary agent commissions (not to exceed 10%), management commissions (not to exceed 10%) actual third party live touring expenses and sales and withholding taxes; provided however, in no event shall Label's share be less than ten (10%) percent of the full gross revenues from each covered contract.

Each accounting statement shall contain a detailed reconciliation of all applicable revenue, the source and each applicable deductible expense.

Artist shall maintain accurate books and records with respect to all Ancillary Revenue activities and transactions. Label shall have the right, upon not less than thirty (30) days prior written notice to inspect Artist's books and records to verify the accuracy of accountings rendered under this paragraph; such inspection to be conducted during normal business hours at the office where such records are maintained. Any audit by Label shall be conducted, if at all, within two (2) years after the date the statement(s) in question were rendered. After the expiration of said two (2) year period, each accounting shall be deemed to be an account stated."

Chapter 6
Summary of Key Negotiation Bullet Points

Each 360/Ancillary Rights agreement is different. Some recording contracts merely include a brief paragraph or two to capture the basic rights. Numerous labels now utilize well drafted, separate (and detailed) agreements covering each primary area of ancillary activity, such as: fan clubs, touring and merchandising. If an artist is presented with separate rights agreements, it is important to link each agreement with the recording contract so that all ancillary rights grants are co-terminous with the Term of the recording agreement. This means that once the record deal expires or terminates, the separate ancillary rights agreements will likewise and simultaneously expire or terminate.

Given the growing prevalence and importance of 360/ancillary rights to both labels and artists, focus must be afforded to these provisions during the negotiation process. Below is a summary of the primary material points of negotiation, which an artist (or artist representative) should seek to attain.

1. Establish a benchmark for the commencement of the label's ancillary rights entitlement; i.e.:
  a. upon the commercial release of the first single
  b. upon the first recording achieving a pre-determined sales level
  c. upon the first recording reaching a pre-determined chart position (i.e. Billboard, Top 50—specific genre—Chart).

2. Obtain an advance for the ancillary rights
    a. non-recoupable, or
    b. recoupable as an additional recording cost.
    c. specify a separate advance for each album or each contract period.

3. Control and administration of the rights
    a. artist to retain full control and administration of their ancillary-rights and activities.
    b. provide the label with a copy of each ancillary activity agreement.
    c. provide a letter of direction to each third party payor to account directly to the label.

4. Label share of Ancillary Revenues
    a. calculate the label share on the basis of net revenues rather than gross.
    b. Option: If gross is required, carve out several "adjusted gross" deductions such as: talent agent commissions, sound and lights and opening acts expenses, literary agent's commissions, management commissions and certain touring expenses. In such cases, the label will most likely demand a "minimum floor" (i.e. twenty (20%) percent of net revenues, but in no event less than ten (10%) percent of gross revenues).
    c. the label share for touring and live engagements should be less than that for other – less expense heavy – ancillary activities, such as merchandising, endorsements, literary and film/T.V. roles. Aim for a maximum label share of ten (10%) percent on live performances and twelve and one half (12.5%) percent to twenty (20%) percent on all other activities.
    d. seek to cap the aggregate label share of payments per contract period. By way of example: "In no event shall the aggregate ancillary revenue payments to Label exceed the sum of Five Hundred Thousand ($500,000) Dollars during any individual contract period."

5. Term
    a. the term of ancillary revenue participation should ideally expire with the expiration of the term of the record deal.

b. if the label requires an extended term for its ancillary share payments, seek to limit that extension to ninety (90) days post-term and restricted to live engagements only (which were contracted during the term).

6. Accountings

a. if an artist has an experienced business manager/CPA, seek to render quarterly or semi-annual accountings and payments to the label for its share of ancillary revenues

b. Option: use reasonable efforts to authorize and direct third party payors to account to and pay the label directly for its share. This is more difficult when the label share is calculated on a net or adjusted gross basis because the payor may not be privy to the actual deductible expenses.

7. Exclusions

a. seek to exclude from ancillary revenue participation activities, areas of businesses in which the artist is already well established, such as acting, a clothing or product line, author, contracts in existence at or prior to the date of execution of the recording agreement, etc.

b. music publishing rights should always be excluded from ancillary rights clauses.

The degree to which an artist will be successful in obtaining many of the concessions above will be a direct result of that artist's marketplace leverage – on a case-by-case basis, as well as internal company policy. Each label generally has its own guidelines for negotiating "gives" and concessions and it's up to the artist's representatives to know what to ask for and which concessions they may reasonably anticipate securing.

Conclusion

For better or worse, 360/ancillary rights deals are now music industry standard in virtually all new artist recording contracts. They are also becoming points for negotiation when mid-level artists enter into new recording pacts with major and mini-major labels. Since 2004, sales of physical CDs have continuously declined. Beginning in 2013, sales of digital singles and albums have likewise begun to decline from prior peak years (down 9% in 2014 for albums and down 12% for singles). While there is and has been no decrease in consumer appetite and consumption for recorded music, trends indicate that an increasing number of music fans are now listening to their music via digital subscription (free and fee based) services such as Sirius/XM satellite, Pandora, Spotify, i-Heart Radio, Rhapsody, Xbox Music Service, Google Play and Beats Music. On demand streaming services revenues increased fifty four (54%) percent in 2014 over 2013, with total streams increasing from 106 billion in 2013 to 164 billion. Some industry researchers predict that by 2017, on demand streaming services will see 1.7 billion users with 125 million paying subscribers.

Total physical and digital album sales declined by eleven (11%) percent in 2014 to 257 million units.

With this bleak but true financial trend and near term forecast, it is evident that traditional record companies will continue to face dwindling revenues with a sales model based primarily on the sale of recorded music. As a path for survival, record labels have invested heavily in digital streaming services, cut catalog deals with industry leading online music portals (receiving multi-million dollar advances) and expanded their artist generated revenue streams with the inclusion of 360/ancillary rights provisions in most new contracts.

The additional challenge for labels, who have secured ancillary rights from their artists is how to administer and collect on those rights. Labels today are facing an inverse reality: they are acquiring more rights from artists and have fewer and steadily decreasing staff to administer and enforce (i.e. collect and monetize) those rights. Hence, most labels do not have the personnel resources to police their rights, and fail to do so unless and until an artist achieves notable commercial success and undertakes major concert tours, merchandising deals, endorsements and other entertainment industry related revenue generating activities.

For the artist, new and established, the 360/ancillary rights agreements represent an unwanted incursion into their financial pie; an area that historically was "off limits" to the labels. This new participant in the artist's expense stream is generally a passive payee because the agreements don't require the label to render any additional services, directly solicit or create new revenue opportunities or assist the artist in fulfilling their obligations under their third party deals. The quid pro quo being, if a record company invests significant sums in developing, promoting or enhancing an artist's career or brand, then they should share in the total financial pie created as a direct or indirect result of their "at risk" investment.

It is therefore incumbent on artists and their business and legal representatives to fully understand the material terms and conditions contained in 360/ancillary rights clauses and agreements and to be knowledgeable and fore-armed with negotiating strategies to reduce the financial impact on the artist. Keep in mind that it's extremely difficult to motivate an artist to embark on a tour knowing that after all is said and done, they may net less from their performances than their managers, record company and talent agent (when commissions and label shares are calculated on the basis of 10% - 25% of the gross earnings being payable to each recipient). Given the fact that most artists will never receive a royalty check from their record label based on music sales, focus must be given on ways to enhance and maximize ancillary revenue from song-writing and music publishing, touring, merchandising, endorsements, book deals, film and T.V. appearances and consumer products lines;

while minimizing the costs, commissions and deductions connected to these ancillary income streams. Soon, these so-called "ancillary" revenue streams will become the "primary" revenue streams and music sales will become the ancillary bucket.

Remember that the phrase "MUSIC BUSINESS" consists of two equally important words and the most creative, commercially successful artists will need to pay equal attention to the business side of their careers if they are to survive and excel creatively and financially.

Appendix
Sample Contracts and Clauses

Appendix 1

SHINING STAR, L.L.C.
123 Broadway
Suite A
New York, New York   10016

Dated as of January 2, 2015

Mr. Jeffrey Waters
Midnight Moon, Inc.
789 Seventh Avenue
Suite B203
New York, New York   10019

Re: **Profit Split Joint Venture Agreement**

Gentlemen:

Shining Star, L.L.C. represented by Martin Hugger ("Star") hereby engages Midnight Moon, Inc., on behalf of Jeffrey Waters ("Moon") to furnish on an exclusive basis during the Term hereof, the Entertainment Services of Jeffrey Waters ("Artist") to the Venture between the above-referenced parties as described herein as follows:

WHEREAS, Star and Moon have an agreement with Waterford ("Digital Distributor") and TBD ("Physical Distributor" both hereinafter referred to as "Distributor") for the exploitation of Assets (as herein defined) and the parties have and desire to enter into an agreement to share equally in the profits solely with respect to Artist's Entertainment Services and with respect to the exploitation of the Assets.

WHEREAS, the parties hereto wish to collaborate and work together as joint venture participants for the purpose of recording, producing, distributing, promoting, selling, licensing and otherwise exploiting music and recordings and other intellectual property created and/or performed by the Artist;

NOW, THEREFORE, the parties hereto agree to create and operate during the Term hereof a joint venture to create, manage, control, administer and exploit the Assets (as defined below) and the products of the Artist's services (hereinafter the "Venture").

1. Obligations of the Parties
   A.   During the Term (as defined below) of this Agreement, the Artist shall render his exclusive services as a recording and performing artist, producer, songwriter, arranger, engineer, musician, vocalist, actor, author and entertainer (collectively the "Entertainment Services").
   B.   Star shall provide the non-exclusive personal services of Hugger to assist with the production of all master recordings made hereunder and to supervise and oversee the day-to-day management of the Venture.

2. Term
   (a)   The Term of the Agreement and the Venture shall commence as of the date hereof and shall continue until the sooner of (i) twenty-four (24) months from the date hereof; or (ii) eighteen (18) months after the date of initial commercial "street date" release of the Album in the United States (the "Term").
   (b)   Upon the expiration of the Term, the Venture shall continue to own and administer the Assets and the Album and to exploit such property, subject to the accounting provisions set forth in paragraph "5" below.

3. Profit Share
   (a)   Star and Moon will each be entitled to receive and shall be paid fifty (50%) percent of all Venture net profits (as defined in paragraph 5 below) ("Profit Shares").

4. <u>Copyright Ownership</u>: Expressly subject to the conditions and requirements set forth below in this paragraph 4, Moon shall assign to Star, in perpetuity, fifty percent (50) ownership of its interest in all Master Recordings by Artist (and other intellectual property [e.g. artwork]) delivered pursuant to the album entitled "Let It Rain" Featuring Jeffrey Waters (the "Album"), and the copyrights thereto, including the copyrights in the underlying musical compositions (collectively, the "Assets"). Such conditional assignments of the Master Recordings and the copyrights thereto (collectively, the "Copyright Interests") shall be subject to the following:

(a) The Venture shall retain all administration rights with respect to all such Master Recordings and the copyrights thereto;

(b) Full and timely performance of all of Moon's material obligations hereunder subject to the period of thirty (30) days to cure any failure to perform any material obligations following receipt of Star's written notice to Moon of such failure;

(c) Star will maintain a security interest in Moon's copyright interest in the Master Recordings and the copyrights thereto in the form of a copyright mortgage;

(d) Moon grants to the Venture a perpetual, exclusive license to exploit the rights in the Assets and the copyrights thereto subject to the obligation to pay the Profit Shares pursuant to the terms set forth herein; and

(e) Each party will execute and deliver to the other any documents as may be reasonably required to demonstrate and/or effectuate the intent and purposes of this Agreement.

5. <u>Accountings</u>

(a) Accountings as to Profit Share accruing or which otherwise would have accrued hereunder shall be made by the Venture to Star and Moon, quarter-annually, on or before thirty (30) days after the close of each calendar quarter or such other accounting periods as the parties may in general adopt, but in no case less frequently than quarter-annually, together with payment of accrued Profit Shares, if any, earned by the exploitation of Assets and Artist's Entertainment Services during such preceding quarter-annual period, less other recoupable and/or deductible amounts hereunder (if any).

(b)   Amounts payable to each respective party hereunder in connection with the exploitation of the Assets, the Album and the Artist's Entertainment Services hereunder shall be computed in the same national currency as is paid or credited by its Distributor and/or licensees and shall be paid at the same rate of exchange as is paid, and shall be subject to any taxes applicable to royalties remitted by or received from foreign sources, provided, however, that amounts payable on Records sold outside the United States shall not be due and payable until payment therefor has been received in the United States in United States Dollars.

(c)   (i)   All accounting statements rendered to Star and Moon, respectively shall be binding upon the party receiving the accounting statement and not subject to any objection for any reason unless specific objection in writing, stating the basis thereof, is given within three (3) years from the date rendered. Failure to make specific objection within said time period will be deemed approval of such statement.

(ii) The parties shall use their best efforts to have the Venture's Distributor provide accounting statements directly to both parties with regard to the Master Recordings.

(d)   Both parties shall have the right at their own expense to audit the Venture's and the other party's books and records only as the same pertain to the exploitation of the Assets and the Artist's Entertainment Services and calculation of Profit Share hereunder (including, without limitation, returns of Records and the liquidation of reserves) on which amounts are payable for the six (6) semi -annual accounting periods prior to the other party's receipt of written notice from the party which desires to audit such books and records. Such auditing party may make such an examination for a particular statement only once, and only within three (3) years after the date when said statement is rendered under paragraph 4(a) above. Such audit shall be conducted during usual business hours, and at the party being audited regular place of business in the United States where that party keeps the books and records to be examined. Such audit shall be conducted by an independent certified public accountant.

(e)   The parties acknowledge that the books and records contain confidential trade information. Neither party nor its representatives shall at any time communicate to others or use on behalf of any other person any facts or information obtained as a result of such examination of such books and records, unless such disclosure is required pursuant to an order of a court of competent jurisdiction. In the event such disclosure is so ordered, the party receiving said order, shall notify the other party in writing promptly following receipt of such order.

(f)   Neither party will have the right to bring an action against the other or the Venture in connection with any accounting or payments hereunder unless it commences the suit within three and one-half (3-1/2) years from the date such statement of accounting or such payment was rendered. If the party commences suit on any controversy or claim concerning accountings rendered under this agreement, the scope of the proceeding will be limited to determination of the amount due for the accounting periods concerned, and the court will have no authority to consider any other issues or award any relief except recovery of any Profit Share found owing. Either party's recovery of any such amounts will be the sole remedy available to that party by reason of any claim related to accountings. Without limiting the generality of the preceding sentence, neither party will not have any right to seek termination of this agreement or avoid the performance of its obligations under it by reason of any such claim. Notwithstanding the foregoing, in the event any court determines fraud, gross negligence or willful misconduct on the part of either party in connection with any such claim, and such determination is not overturned or reversed, the limitations set forth in this paragraph 5(f) shall not apply.

(g)   The parties hereby authorize and direct the other and the Venture to withhold from any monies due the other any part thereof required by the United States Internal Revenue Service and/or any other governmental authority to be withheld, and to pay same to the United States Internal Revenue Service and/or such other authority. Each party shall provide the other with a copy of any notice received from the applicable governmental authority requiring it to withhold such monies and pay such monies to the applicable governmental authority.

(h)   Capital Accounts: The parties hereto acknowledge and agree that while they are not forming a separate legal entity ("Venture") (e.g., a corporation, partnership or a limited liability company) to operate and exploit the Assets, solely for accounting and federal income tax purposes the Venture will be treated as a partnership. Accordingly, solely for purposes of this paragraph, each of Moon and Star is hereinafter sometimes referred to as a "Partner." The Label shall maintain a separate capital account (a "Capital Account") for each Partner. Such Capital Account shall be increased by (i) the amount of cash and the fair market value of any other asset contributed by any such Partner to the Label pursuant to this agreement, and (ii) such Partner's allocable share of Capital Profits (as defined below) and any special allocations of income or gain; and decreased by (A) the amount of cash and the fair market value of any property distributed to such Partner by the Venture pursuant to this agreement (excluding any guaranteed payments to the Partners) and (B) such Partner's allocable share of loss and any special allocations of loss or deduction. Amounts loaned to the Venture hereunder shall not constitute contributions. It is the intention of the Partners that each Partner's Capital Account shall be maintained in accordance with the rules set forth in Section 1.704- 1(b)(2)(iv) of the Treasury Regulations promulgated under Section 704(b) of the Code, and this provision shall be interpreted consistently therewith. The parties agree that to date, neither party has made any capital contribution.

> (i) <u>Losses</u>: One hundred percent (100%) of losses, if any, incurred by the Venture, shall be allocated be allocated among the Partners in proportion to their partnership interests to the extent of their positive Capital Account balances.

> (j) <u>Capital Profits</u>:
> (i) Capital Profits will be allocated first to each party to the extent losses were allocated to that party under subparagraph (i) above as a result of the limitation of each party's Capital Account (with the intent of maintaining the Partners' 50 / 50 interests); then
> (ii) Capital Profits will be allocated to the Partners based on their ownership percentages (i.e., fifty percent (50%) to Star and fifty percent (50%) to Moon).

> (k) <u>Tax Matters</u>:
> (i) Star shall be the Venture's Tax Matters Partner under the Code "ABC"). The ABC shall cause the applicable partnership tax returns and IRS Form 1065 with Schedule K-l to be prepared and delivered in a timely manner to the Partners (but in no event later than one

hundred eighty (180) days after the end of the applicable fiscal year (i.e. December 31), unless Moon and Star subsequently mutually agree that any such tax filings are not necessary, or the parties agree to treat each other as independent contractor status.

(ii) Proper and complete books of account of the affairs of the Venture as a partnership shall be kept under the supervision of the ABC at the principal office of the ABC. Such books shall be open to inspection by any Partner, at any reasonable time, upon reasonable notice, during normal business hours.

(l) Capital Account Deficit: No Partner shall be required to restore any negative balance in its Capital Account.

(m) Capital Profits" shall mean Venture Profits without reduction for the reserve for anticipated Record Expenses.

6. Warranties and Representations; Indemnity

(a) (i) Moon is authorized, empowered and able to enter into and fully perform Moon's obligations under this agreement. Neither this agreement nor the fulfillment thereof by any party infringes upon the rights of any person or entity. Moon is a Corporation duly organized, existing and in good standing under the laws of the State of New York. The party executing this agreement on Moon's behalf is an authorized representative of Moon, duly authorized to sign on Moon's behalf.

(ii) Star is authorized, empowered and able to enter into and fully perform Star's obligations under this agreement. Neither this agreement nor the fulfillment thereof by any party infringes upon the rights of any person or entity. Star is a Corporation organized, existing and in good standing under the laws of the State of New York. The party executing this agreement on Star's behalf is an authorized representative of Star, duly authorized to sign on Star's behalf.

(b) Moon agrees to and does hereby indemnify, save and hold Star harmless of and from any and all liability, loss, damage, cost or expense (including reasonable third-party attorneys' fees) arising out of any third party claim arising out of or connected with any breach of this agreement or which is inconsistent with any of the warranties or representations made by Moon in this agreement, provided that said claim has been settled with Moon's written consent, not to be unreasonably withheld, or has been reduced to final adverse judgment by a court of competent jurisdiction, and agrees to reimburse Star promptly following Star's demand for any payment made or incurred by Star with respect to any liability or claim to which the foregoing indemnity applies. Notwithstanding anything to the contrary contained herein, Star shall have the right to settle without Moon's consent any claim involving sums of Seven Thousand Five Hundred Dollars ($7,500) or less (or involving claims of ownership or exploitation of intellectual property), and this indemnity shall apply in full to any claim so settled; if Moon does not consent to any settlement proposed by Star for an amount in excess of Seven Thousand Five Hundred Thousand Dollars ($7,500), Star shall have the right to settle such claim without Moon's consent, and this indemnity shall apply in full to any claim so settled, unless Moon obtains a surety bond from a surety acceptable to Star in its sole discretion, with Star as a beneficiary, assuring Star of prompt payment of all expenses, losses and damages (including reasonable attorneys' fees) which Star may incur as a result of said claim. Pending final determination of any involving such alleged breach or failure, Star may withhold sums due Moon hereunder in an amount reasonably consistent claim with the amount of such claim, unless Moon obtains a surety bond from a surety acceptable to Star in its sole discretion, with Star as a beneficiary, in an amount reasonably consistent with the amount of such claim. If no action is filed within twelve (12) months following the date on which such claim was first received by Star, Star shall release all sums withheld in connection with such claim, unless Star, in its reasonable business judgment, believes an action will be filed within the reasonably foreseeable future. Notwithstanding the foregoing, if after such release by Star of sums withheld in connection with a particular claim, such claim is reasserted, then Star's rights under this paragraph 6(b) will apply ab initio in full force and effect. Star will give Moon prompt notice of any lawsuit instituted with respect to such a claim, and Moon shall have the right to participate in the defense thereof with counsel of Moon's choice and at Moon's expense provided, however, that Star shall have the right at all times to maintain control of the conduct of the defense.

(c) Star agrees to and does hereby indemnify, save and hold Moon harmless of and from any and all liability, loss, damage, cost or expense (including reasonable third-party attorneys' fees) arising out of any third party claim arising out of or connected with any breach of this agreement or which is inconsistent with any of the warranties or representations made by Star in this agreement, provided that said claim has been settled with Star's written consent, not to be unreasonably withheld, or has been reduced to final adverse judgment by a court of competent jurisdiction, and agrees to reimburse Moon promptly following Moon's demand for any payment made or incurred by Moon with respect to any liability or claim to which the foregoing indemnity applies. Notwithstanding anything to the contrary contained herein, Moon shall have the right to settle without Star's consent any claim involving sums of Seven Thousand Five Hundred Dollars ($7,500) or less (or involving claims of ownership or exploitation of intellectual property), and this indemnity shall apply in full to any claim so settled; if Star does not consent to any settlement proposed by Moon for an amount in excess of Seven Thousand Five Hundred Thousand Dollars ($7,500), Moon shall have the right to settle such claim without Star's consent, and this indemnity shall apply in full to any claim so settled, unless Star obtains a surety bond from a surety acceptable to Moon in its sole discretion, with Moon as a beneficiary, assuring Moon of prompt payment of all expenses, losses and damages (including reasonable attorneys' fees) which Moon may incur as a result of said claim. Pending final determination of any claim involving such alleged breach or failure, Moon may withhold sums due Star hereunder in an amount reasonably consistent with the amount of such claim, unless Star obtains a surety bond from a surety acceptable to Moon in its sole discretion, with Moon as a beneficiary, in an amount reasonably consistent with the amount of such claim. If no action is filed within twelve (12) months following the date on which such claim was first received by Moon, Moon shall release all sums withheld in connection with such claim, unless Moon, in its reasonable business judgment, believes an action will be filed within the reasonably foreseeable future. Notwithstanding the foregoing, if after such release by Moon of sums withheld in connection with a particular claim, such claim is reasserted, then Moon's rights under this paragraph 6(b) will apply ab initio in full force and effect. Moon will give Star prompt notice of any lawsuit instituted with respect to such a claim, and Star shall have the right to participate in the defense thereof with counsel of Star's choice and at Star's expense provided, however, that Moon shall have the right at all times to maintain control of the conduct of the defense.

7. Star/Moon's Logo

(a) During and after the Term, Star and Moon's logo or other trade symbol designated by Moon and Star (the "Symbol") shall be equally displayed on all product covers, advertisements and marketing materials and ads wherever and whenever the Moon or Star designated logo appears (e.g., on the packaging of Records, in U.S. trade and consumer advertisements, in point-of-purchase, etc.). For the avoidance of doubt, Star and Moon's logo shall also be included as a so-called "chyron" for Audio-Visual Recordings hereunder. The size and placement of the Symbol shall be the same for Star and Moon.

(b) The registration and maintenance of the Symbol shall be each party's respective sole responsibility, and at each party's sole expense.

8. Definitions

All capitalized terms not specifically defined herein shall have the meaning set forth in the Artist Agreement.

(a) "Revenues"; For any period, the sum of (i) one hundred percent (100%) of the monies actually received by or credited to either party in the United States solely attributable to the exploitation of Assets including, without limitation, sales of Records derived from Artist's Masters and other exploitations (including, without limitation, monies received in connection with the exploitation of Artist's Masters through ancillary distribution channels, Mobile Materials, Voice Messages and advertising revenue derived from the Artist Website [if any]).

(b) "Charges": For any period calculated in accordance with U.S. GAAP for such period, without duplication:
- (i) all out of pocket, third-party costs paid or accrued to non-affiliated third parties by either party in connection with the recording, production, clearance and exploitation of the Album and Master Recordings;
- (ii) all legal and accounting fees, registration fees;
- (iii) all manufacturing, artwork preparation and production costs in connection with exploitation of the Album and Master Recordings;

(iv) all other expenses in connection with exploitation of the Album and Master Recordings properly charged against income in accordance with U.S. GAAP;

(v) any advances, royalties and the like paid pursuant producers, engineers, re-mixers, outside artists, music publishers; and

(vi) all manufacturing, packaging and shipping costs; and

(vii) all mutually approved Venture general and administrative costs.

(c) "U.S. GAAP": Generally accepted accounting principles set forth in the opinions and pronouncements of the Accounting Principles Board of the Institute of Certified Public Accountants and statements and pronouncements of the Financial Accounting Standards Board or such other statements by such other entity as may be approved by a significant segment of the accounting profession, in each case consistent with the manner in which the same are applied to the financial statements of Star.

(d) "Profit": Revenues less all Charges.

(e) "Master", "Recording", "Master Recording": Any recording of sound, whether or not coupled with a visual image, by any method and on any substance or material, whether now or hereafter known, including Audio-Visual Recordings, intended for reproduction in the form of Phonograph Records, or otherwise.

(f) "Records", "Phonograph Records": Any device now or hereafter known, on or by which sound may be recorded and reproduced, which is manufactured or distributed primarily for home and/or consumer and/or jukebox use and/or use on or in means of transportation including "sight and sound" devices or Audio-Visual Devices.

(g) "Person": Any individual, corporation, partnership, association, or other entity, or the legal successors or representative of any of the foregoing.

(h) "Net Sales": Gross billings less returns and credits (other than cash rebates and discounts), and less value added and similar taxes to the extent included within the price of Records concerned. Gross billings shall mean monies actually received by or credited to either party for Records shipped for sale in the United States.

(i) "Album": One album, sold in a single package currently entitled "Right Now".

9. Miscellaneous

(a)   Except as provided herein for accounting and federal tax purposes, nothing herein contained shall constitute a partnership between, or joint venture by, the parties hereto, or constitute either party the agent of the other, and neither party shall become liable for any representation, act or omission of the other which is contrary to the provisions of this paragraph.

(b)   This writing sets forth the entire understanding between the parties hereto with respect to the subject matter hereof, and no modification, amendment or waiver of this document shall be binding upon either party hereto unless confirmed by a written instrument which is signed by an authorized signatory of each such party. No waiver of any provision of, or waiver of a default under this agreement nor any failure to exercise rights hereunder shall prejudice the rights of either party thereafter, nor shall it form precedent for the future.

(c)   Notwithstanding anything expressed or implied herein to the contrary, neither party exercising of any of their rights, or pursuing any remedies under this agreement shall not act as a waiver or an exclusion of their rights or remedies hereunder.

(d) All notices required to be sent to either party at its address first mentioned herein, and all Profit Share accounting statements and payments and any and all notices to shall be sent to the address first mentioned herein, or such other address as each party respectively may hereafter designate by notice in writing to the other. All notices sent under this agreement shall be in writing and, except for Profit Share accounting statements shall be sent by overnight mail or registered or certified mail, return receipt requested, and the day of mailing of any such notice shall be deemed the date of the giving thereof (except notices of change of address, the date of which shall be the date of receipt by the receiving party). A courtesy copy of all notices to Star shall be served upon Sidney Weather, Esq., Weather & Storm, L.LC., 411 Lincoln Street, Suite 456, New York, New York 10016. A courtesy copy of all notices to Moon shall be served upon Jack Daniels, Esq., Daniels & Scotch, L.L.C., 755 East 42nd Street, New York, New York 10022.

(e)   THIS AGREEMENT IS ENTERED INTO IN THE STATE OF NEW YORK AND SHALL BE CONSTRUED IN

ACCORDANCE WITH THE LAWS OF NEW YORK APPLICABLE TO CONTRACTS ENTERED INTO AND TO BE WHOLLY PERFORMED THEREIN (WITHOUT GIVING EFFECT TO ANY CONFLICT OF LAWS OR PRINCIPLES UNDER NEW YORK LAW). THE PARTIES AGREE THAT ANY ACTION, SUIT OR PROCEEDING BASED UPON ANY MATTER, CLAIM OR CONTROVERSY ARISING HEREUNDER OR RELATING HERETO SHALL BE BROUGHT SOLELY IN THE STATE COURTS OF OR THE FEDERAL COURT IN THE STATE AND COUNTY OF NEW YORK; EXCEPT THAT IN THE EVENT EITHER PARTY IS SUED OR JOINED IN ANY OTHER COURT OR IN ANY OTHER FORUM IN RESPECT OF ANY MATTER WHICH MAY GIVE RISE TO A CLAIM BY EITHER PARTY HEREUNDER, THE PARTIES HERETO CONSENT TO THE JURISDICTION OF SUCH COURT OR FORUM OVER ANY CLAIM WHICH MAY BE ASSERTED BY STAR THEREIN. THE PARTIES HERETO IRREVOCABLY WAIVE ANY OBJECTION TO THE VENUE OF THE ABOVE-MENTIONED COURTS, INCLUDING ANY CLAIM THAT SUCH ACTION, SUIT OR PROCEEDING HAS BEEN BROUGHT IN AN INCONVENIENT FORUM. ANY PROCESS IN ANY ACTION, SUIT OR PROCEEDING ARISING OUT OF OR RELATING TO THIS AGREEMENT MAY, AMONG OTHER METHODS PERMITTED BY LAW, BE SERVED UPON MOON BY DELIVERING OR MAILING THE SAME IN ACCORDANCE WITH PARAGRAPH 10 (d) HEREOF.

(f)   Each party hereto understands and acknowledges that this agreement is a valid and binding legal document which affects the legal and financial interests of each party. Each party acknowledges that it has had ample opportunity to read this Agreement and that its principal understands the terms and conditions set forth in this Agreement. Each party hereto hereby acknowledges that it has had an opportunity to obtain independent legal counsel in connection with the execution of this Agreement and each party further acknowledges that it has either obtained such independent legal counselor has voluntarily waived its right to do so.

(g)   Without limitation of any other rights and remedies, if either party hereto fails to fulfill any of its material obligations hereunder, then the other party may, at its election, suspend its obligations hereunder for a number of days equal to the number of days between the date on which the delinquent party failed to fulfill its material obligations under this Agreement and the date on which it actually fulfills such material obligation(s). If any such failure exceeds ninety (90) days, in addition to its other rights and remedies, the aggrieved party may, at its election, demand reimbursement from the other party of all monies theretofore paid by it under this Agreement and/or terminate this Agreement by written notice and upon such termination the Venture shall terminate and neither party shall have any further obligations hereunder except with respect to accountings.

(h)   This agreement shall not be construed against either party as the drafter, it being agreed that this agreement has been drafted jointly by the parties.

(i)   This document may be signed in counterparts, and may be executed and delivered by facsimile, which when taken together will have the same effect as if signed in its original by both parties.

(j)   Either party may, at its election, assign this agreement or any of its rights hereunder to any subsidiary, affiliate or division, or any entity that is owned or controlled (in whole or in part) by the principal of either party, or to any entity that merges its assets with those of a party hereto.

Very truly yours,
SHINING STAR, L.L.C.

By: _____

ACCEPTED AND AGREED TO:

MIDNIGHT MOON, INC.

By:_____

<u>Exhibit "A"</u>

Inducement Letter

In order to induce Shining Star, L.L.C., ("Star") to enter into the foregoing agreement ("Agreement") with Midnight Moon, Inc., ("Moon") dated January 2, 2015, the undersigned hereby: (a) acknowledges that he has read and is familiar with all of the terms and conditions of the Agreement; (b) assents to the execution of the Agreement and agrees to be bound by the terms and conditions thereof, including but not limited to each and every provision of the Agreement that relate to him in any way, directly or indirectly, the services to be rendered thereunder by him and restrictions imposed upon him in accordance with the provisions of the Agreement, and hereby guarantees to Artist the full and faithful performance of all the terms and conditions of the Agreement by him, and by Company; and (c) acknowledges and agrees that Artist shall be under no obligation to make any payments to the undersigned for or in connection with this inducement or for or in connection with the services rendered by him or in connection with the fulfillment of his obligations pursuant to the Agreement and the rights granted to Artist thereunder, and that he shall look solely to Company for payment of any sums due to him in connection with his services under the Agreement.

_____

Jeffrey Waters

Exhibit "B"

Inducement Letter

In order to induce Midnight Moon, Inc., ("Moon") to enter into the foregoing agreement ("Agreement") with Shining Star, L.L.C., ("Star") dated January 2, 2015, the undersigned hereby: (a) acknowledges that he has read and is familiar with all of the terms and conditions of the Agreement; (b) assents to the execution of the Agreement and agrees to be bound by the terms and conditions thereof, including but not limited to each and every provision of the Agreement that relate to him in any way, directly or indirectly, the services to be rendered thereunder by him and restrictions imposed upon him in accordance with the provisions of the Agreement, and hereby guarantees to Artist the full and faithful performance of all the terms and conditions of the Agreement by him, and by Company; and (c) acknowledges and agrees that Artist shall be under no obligation to make any payments to the undersigned for or in connection with this inducement or for or in connection with the services rendered by him or in connection with the fulfillment of his obligations pursuant to the Agreement and the rights granted to Artist thereunder, and that he shall look solely to Company for payment of any sums due to him in connection with his services under the Agreement.

_____

Martin Hugger

Appendix 2

Sample Ancillary Rights Clause
(Extracted from an Exclusive Recording Agreement)

NON-RECORD PARTICIPATION

   (a) Company will be entitled to receive and you hereby irrevocably grant to Company twenty percent (20%) (the "Ancillary Share") of all "Net Royalty Receipts" (as defined herein) otherwise payable to you or Artist (or to a third party on your and/or the Artist's behalf) during the Term or pursuant to any agreements, commitments or engagements entered into or secured during the Term in connection with the following (all such monies are referred to herein as "Covered Revenues," and the activities referred in clauses (i) through (v) below are sometimes referred to herein as "Covered Activities") whether the Covered Revenues under such agreements are received during or after the Term, provided that income derived from music publishing shall be excluded: (i) services rendered by the Artist as an actor or performer (in any and all media, including without limitation film and television), the preceding notwithstanding, excluding all "Net Royalty Receipts" accruing to Artist from his participation in the stage production "Behind the Pulpit", (ii) endorsements and strategic partnerships, (iii) non-fiction books, magazines and other non-fiction publishing materials, (iv) website revenues, and (v) games, including, without limitation, video games and as otherwise may be required pursuant to the Distribution Agreement provided that in the event Distributor only agrees to accept a share of Artist's gross monies in connection with Covered Activities then in such event, the foregoing percentage herein shall be deemed to be that required by Distributor in the Distribution Agreement and this agreement shall be conformed therewith in such regard. "Net Royalty Receipts", as used in this paragraph shall mean the gross sums actually received by or credited to Artist in connection with Covered Revenues. Notwithstanding anything to the contrary contained herein, the Ancillary Share shall be calculated pursuant to Distributors standard calculations of Covered Revenues (i.e., after deduction of the same (costs and expenses permitted pursuant to the Distribution Agreement). It is acknowledged and agreed that to the extent Distributor requires a participation in Covered Revenues, the Ancillary Share of Net royalty Receipts in connection with Covered Revenues shall be increased SID as to account for Distributor's Participation, provided that in no event shall said increase exceed an additional fifteen (15%) percent of Artist's Net Royalty Receipts without Artist's prior, written consent. Additionally, you hereby irrevocably grant to Company ten (10%) percent of all gross monies otherwise payable to Artist (or to a third party on Artist's behalf) (the "Ancillary Tour Share") pursuant to any agreements, commitments or engagements entered into or secured during the Term in connection with the Artist's live performance engagements and appearances ("Covered Tour Revenues"). To the extent Distributor requires participation in connection with Artist's live performance engagements and appearances, the Ancillary Tour Share percentage shall be increased so as to account for Distributor's participation therein, provided that in no event shall said increase exceed an additional five (5%) percent of all gross monies otherwise payable to Artist (or to a third party on Artist's behalf) without Artist's prior, written consent.

(b) You will irrevocably direct and will use best reasonable efforts to cause each Person from which you or Artist or any Person receiving revenues on your or Artist's behalf receive Covered Revenues and Covered Tour Revenues ("Third Party"), to account directly to Company for Company's share of such Covered Revenues and) Covered Tour Revenues at the same times and subject to the same accounting terms as apply to accountings to you, Artist and/or the applicable Person receiving Covered Revenues and Covered Tour Revenues on your or Artist's behalf, but no less frequently than quarterly, provided that the failure of said Third Party to do so account and pay Company shall relieve you of the obligation to so account and pay Company its share of Covered Revenues and Covered Tour Revenues as set forth herein. You shall use reasonable efforts to cause all agreements With Third Parties (each, a "Covered Revenue Agreement',) to provide that Company shall have the right to examine each Third Party's books and records with respect to Covered Revenues and Covered Tour Revenues subject to the same terms and limitations as apply to accountings to you, Artist and/or the applicable Person receiving Covered Revenues and Covered Tour Revenues on your or Artist's behalf. You will provide Company with a copy of each Covered Revenue Agreement within ten (10) days after the execution of such agreement.

Appendix 3

Sample Ancillary Rights Clause
(a pro-label approach)

ANCILLARY RIGHTS

(a)   During the Term hereof, Company shall receive an "all-in" royalty (i.e. inclusive and any Distributor share of ancillary participation) of fifty (50%) percent of Artist's "Net Receipts" (as defined below) derived from the exploitation of Artist's services rendered during the Term, substantially negotiated during the Term or within the twelve (12) month period following the Term in connection with all entertainment related endeavors, including but not limited to the following ("Ancillary Revenues"): (i) services as an actor or performer (in any and all media, including without limitation motion picture and television), (ii) live performance and concert engagements (including public stage performances of all kinds, web-casts, sponsorships, television or cable broadcasts, pay-per-view broadcasts, one-nighters, concert tours and the like), (iii) non-fiction books, magazines and other non-fiction publishing materials, (iv) games, including, without limitation, video games, (v) the use or exploitation of Artist's name, voice or likeness in any manner whatsoever, (vi) Artist's services as a personality, endorser or talent within the live entertainment, music, television, film, media and digital media industries, (vii) sponsorships, (viii) strategic partnerships and joint ventures, (ix) music producer services or engineer, (x) disc jockey services, (xi) services as a photographer, (xii) services as a graphic designer, (xiii) services in the fashion industry as a designer or otherwise, and (xiv) services as a songwriter and/or publisher. For the avoidance of doubt and if applicable, Company shall not be entitled to receive Net Receipts for any record royalties, merchandise royalties or publishing royalties paid through Company herein. The term "substantially negotiated" as used herein shall mean that negotiations have proceeded to a point where specific terms of the agreement have been discussed in detail, it being understood that such negotiations will be more than a mere solicitation of interest, but need not have proceeded to the point where an offer has been made. Company shall be entitled to continue to receive and retain its fifty (50%) percent share of Net Receipts for all Ancillary Revenues, for the life of the applicable agreement without regard to the expiration or termination of the Term hereof. Should the Distributor request an ancillary participation; Company's share of Net Receipts shall have a minimum floor of twenty (25%) percent.

(i) In reasonable consultation with Artist, Agreements which are subject to Company's ancillary rights participation shall be facilitated and entered into by Company on behalf of Artist and Artist's entertainment services. It is understood that any contract or agreement entered into by you or your representative in contravention of this Agreement without the express written consent of Company and shall constitute a material breach of contract and you shall indemnify and hold harmless Company from any and all claims, liabilities, damages and costs (including attorneys' fees and court costs) arising out of or pertaining to such unauthorized contract or agreement. Your failure to perform the terms and obligations of any Company agreements which furnishes your services as an entertainer under this paragraph shall constitute a breach of contract and you shall indemnify Company from any loss and against any and all claims, damages, liabilities, costs and expenses, including legal expenses and reasonable counsel fees, arising out of said breach or alleged breach. Company shall forward a copy of all agreements entered into pursuant to this paragraph to Artist upon Artist's written request.

(b) For the purposes of this paragraph, "Net Receipts" shall mean the gross earnings received by Artist and derived from Ancillary Revenues less any bonafide, documented and direct expense actually incurred in connection with such Ancillary revenues, limited to (i) costs of collections,

(ii) reasonable manufacturing costs, and (iii) costs of negotiating and entering into third party agreement with respect to reasonable legal fees for such Ancillary Revenues.

(c) The Company Ancillary Revenues shall be payable when Net Receipts are received by or credited to Artist. Net Receipts shall be deemed to have been received by Artist, and Company shall be entitled to receive the Company Ancillary Revenues thereon, if such Net Receipts are received, directly or indirectly, by Artist or by any other party or entity on or for Artist's behalf, or by any party or entity which furnished Artist's services. Company shall receive all sums payable to Artist under this paragraph and shall account to Artist on a bi-monthly basis. Each statement shall include an itemized breakdown of all exploitations. A Certified Public Accountant on Artist's behalf may, at Company's offices and at Artist's expense, examine Company's books and records relevant to the calculation of Ancillary Revenues solely for the purposes of verifying the accuracy of statements rendered by Company to Artist.

Directory

A. Performing Rights Organizations

ASCAP (American Society of Composers, Authors and Publishers)

One Lincoln Plaza
New York, New York 10023
Phone: 212-621-6000
Fax: 212-621-8453
www.ascap.com

7920 W. Sunset Boulevard
3rd Floor
Los Angeles, California 90046
Phone: 323-883-1000
Fax: 323-883-1049

Two Music Square West
Nashville, Tennessee 37203
Phone: 615-742-5000
Fax: 615-742-5020

420 Lincoln Road – Suite 385
Miami, Florida 33139
Phone: 305-673-3446
Fax: 305-673-2446

8 Cork Street
London, W1S 3LJ England
Phone: 011-44-207-439-0909
Fax: 011-44-207-434-0073

Av Martinez Nadal Hill 623
San Juan, Puerto Rico 00920
Phone: 787-707-0782
Fax: 787-707-0783

950 Joseph E. Lowery Boulevard, NW
Suite 23
Atlanta, Georgia 30318
Phone: 404-685-8699
Fax: 404-685-8701

BMI (Broadcast Music, Inc.)

7 World Trade Center
250 Greenwich Street
New York, New York 10007
Phone: 212-220-3000
www.bmi.com

10 Music Square East
Nashville, Tennessee 37203
Phone: 615-401-2000

1691 Michigan Avenue
Suite 350
Miami Beach, Florida 33139
Phone: 305-673-5148

8730 Sunset Boulevard
3rd Floor W
Los Angeles, California 90069
Phone: 310-659-9109

1250 Ponce de Leon Avenue
San Jose Building
Suite 1008
Santurce, Puerto Rico 00907
Phone: 787-754-6490

84 Harley House
Marylebone Road
London, NW1 5HN, England
Phone: 011-44-207-486-2036

3340 Peachtree Road, NE
Suite 570
Atlanta, Georgia 30326
Phone: 404-261-5151

SESAC (Society of European Songwriters Artists and Composers)

55 Music Square East
Nashville, Tennessee 37203
Phone: 615-320-0055
Fax: 615-963-3527
www.sesac.com

6100 Wilshire Boulevard
Suite 700
Los Angeles, California 90048
Phone: 323-937-3722

981 Joseph E. Lowery Boulevard NW
Suite 111
Atlanta, Georgia 30318
Phone: 404-897-1330

152 West 57th Street
57th Floor
New York, New York 10019
Phone: 212-586-3450
Fax: 212-489-5699

67 Upper Berkeley Street
London, W1H 7QX
Phone: 011-44-207-616-9284
Fax: 011-44-207-563-7029

420 Lincoln Road
Suite 502
Miami, Florida 33139
Phone: 305-534-7500

B. SoundExchange

1121 Fourteenth Street NW
Suite 700
Washington, D.C. 20005
Phone: 202-640-5858
Fax: 202-640-5859
www.soundexchange.com

C. RIAA (Recording Industry Association of America)

1025 F. Street N.W.
10th Floor
Washington, D.C. 20004
Phone: 202-775-0101
www.riaa.com

About the Author

Kendall A. Minter, a native of New York City and graduate and Senior Class President of Flushing High School began his professional path at Cornell University where he participated in the six year combined arts/law program, graduating with a B.A., majoring in Political Science in 1974, and with a J.D. from Cornell Law School in 1976.

Upon his graduation from Cornell Law School, he joined Fairchild Industries as Associate General Counsel and Corporate Representative for Broadcasting. His responsibilities at Fairchild also included general "in House" corporate legal matters, such as employment and consulting agreements, trademarks, real estate and labor. In 1978, Kendall returned to New York City and joined the 56—lawyer firm Burns, Jackson, Miller, Summit & Jacoby as an associate. In 1980, Kendall embarked upon his sole practice career and established the Law Firm of Kendall A. Minter, which eventually opened affiliated offices in Los Angeles and London.

In 1984, Kendall joined the law firm of Barnes, Wood, Williams and Rafalsky as counsel, where he remained until establishing Minter & Gay in 1987. Minter & Gay was a boutique law firm which specialized in entertainment, sports and labor law. Based in the Wall Street district, the firm grew to nine attorneys with an internationally diverse clientele. In September 1992, Kendall merged his practice into the firm of Phillips, Nizer, Benjamin, Krim & Balon as counsel. In early 1995, Kendall relocated to Atlanta and joined the firm of Sales Goodloe & Golden, as counsel, where he established and developed an entertainment department. Kendall has also been Of Counsel to the New York City entertainment law firm Rudolph & Beer.

In 2004, Kendall established Minter & Associates, L.L.C. in Atlanta, Georgia and subsequently established an Of Counsel affiliation with regional law firm Gibson & Behman, P.C. Minter & Associates, L.L.C. is a boutique law firm which represents a diverse international clientele in the areas of entertainment, corporate, intellectual property, sports and new media matters.

Kendall is a co-founder and inaugural Executive Director of the Black Entertainment and Sports Lawyers Association (BESLA) and currently serves on its Advisory Board. He also serves on the Board of Directors of Rhythm & Blues Foundation, is a former Chairman and is currently the Chairman Emeritus of the organization. He is a member of the Board and General Counsel of the Living Legends Foundation and is a member of the Board of Directors of Sound Exchange, Inc.

Kendall has also served extended terms as a director of the American Youth Hostels and the 100 Black Men. He was an adjunct professor at Benjamin Cardozo School of Law, currently teaches Copyright and Music Publishing at Georgia State University and is a frequent lecturer for the Practicing Law Institute and numerous other organizations, as well as being a frequent contributor and columnist for several music trade publications.

Kendall is listed in Who's Who in America, Who's Who in American Law, Who's Who in Entertainment, Who's Who in The East and Who's Who amongst Black Americans and he has been inducted into the Knights of Malta, O.S.J. A sampling of Mr. Minter's varied clients, past and present, includes Archbishop Desmond Tutu, Shabba Ranks, Lena Horne, Roy Ayers, Musiq Soulchild, Jermaine Dupri, Najee, Miriam Makeba, Hugh Masekela, Third World, Bunny Wailer, The Government of Jamaica, The Backstreet Boys, Ying Yang Twins, Donell Jones, Jagged Edge, Cassandra Wilson, Teddy Riley, Freddie Jackson, former WBO Heavyweight Champion Ray Mercer, Cameo, Silk, The Fat Boys, Peter Tosh, Ashanti, Onyx, Nat Robinson and First Priority Music, Milk Dee,

M C Lyte, Heavy D & The Boyz, Mad Cobra, Mtume, Kirk Franklin, Fred Hammond, Bishop Eddie Long and New Birth Missionary Baptist Church, Juanita Bynum, Arrow Records (Dr. Creflo Dollar), Pastor Dewey Smith and Greater Traveler's Rest Baptist Church, Montell Jordan and Victory World Church and numerous others.

CPSIA information can be obtained at www.ICGtesting.com
Printed in the USA
LVOW01s1115020615

440847LV00028B/348/P

9 780996 179003